THE NATURAL CAT

THE NATURAL CAT

A HOLISTIC GUIDE FOR FINICKY OWNERS

BY

Anitra Frazier

WITH NORMA ECKROATE

Foreword by Richard H. Pitcairn, D.V.M., Ph.D.
Veterinary Columnist for *Prevention* Magazine

Illustrated by Nancy Lou Gahan

Published in San Francisco by
HARBOR PUBLISHING

Distributed by G. P. Putnam's Sons

Text Designer: Marie Carluccio
Copyeditor: Linda Purrington
Compositor: Abracadabra
Text Printer and Binder: Fairfield Graphics
Jacket/Cover Printer: Alithochrome
Jacket/Cover Illustration: Lowell Herrero
Text Illustrations: Nancy Lou Gahan

Paperbound/ISBN 0-936602-13-9
Hardbound/ISBN 0-936602-12-0

For information contact Harbor Publishing,
1668 Lombard Street, San Francisco, California 94123.

Printed in the United States of America.

*Dedicated to Carole Wilbourn,
whose imagination and trust changed my life
and whose courage and sensitivity
inspired me.*

Acknowledgments

Phyllis Levy, the guiding light who cheered us on

Ephraim London, defender of helpless pussycats

Doctors of Veterinary Medicine, healers and teachers: Dr. Paul Rowan, Dr. Leo Camuti, Dr. Robert J. Perper, Dr. Edward S. Kepner, and Dr. Richard H. Pitcairn

Terry Gruber, Louise Anderson, Mark McCauley, Don Padgett, J. David Stites, and Ellen Stock Stern

And the owners who asked and the cats who taught, especially: Clarence, our editor; Priscilla, inspiration; Florence, domesticity; Giggles, force feeding; Patrick, kidney diet; Marshmallow, pilling; Shiam, colitis; Purr, instinct; Mokie, cystitis; and Gilda and Raoul, devotion.

Contents

Foreword

This is a very special book. It is written by a woman who was willing to put aside a mass of opinion and ignorance and find out for herself the truth about cats.

What strikes me as her greatest contribution (besides a wealth of practical and useful information) is her approach toward understanding. Rather than letting herself be captivated by ideas and images passed on by many sources, she determined to find out firsthand how to care for cats—by asking the animals themselves.

I am reminded of a conversation that took place some years ago between the author J. Allen Boone and Mojave Dan, a desert hermit who had close communion with animals. As he wrote in his fascinating book, *Kinship with All Life,* Boone had been struggling to find out the real truth about the nature of a remarkable dog who was his companion. So he put the issue to his friend Dan. After a long silence, Dan's cogent reply was "There's facts about dogs, and there's opinions about them. The dogs have the facts, and the humans have the opinions. . . . If you want facts about a dog, always get them straight from the dog. If you want opinions, get them from the human."

Much of what Anitra Frazier has learned about cats has come in just such a way, and she has reaped a wealth of information about them. Her book invites you to travel the same road. As you read it, you can see how she evolved the process of watching cats without a screen of preconceptions. This kind of learning does not end.

There is another hidden value in all of this. Many people have learned through relating to animals what it is to care for and accept responsibility for another being. All the basic elements of relationship are there—the same elements found in relationship with a friend, husband or wife, child, or even a plant. If one can discover how to relate fully to an animal, without exploitation, with real care and concern for its welfare and continued physical and psychological well-being, then one can relate to anyone. The skills involved are universal.

Many people have found in themselves a compassion they did not know existed, by relating to an animal in their life. This potential is meant to be extended to all relationships. Some, however, focus their affections on only one or two animals, and in so doing become withdrawn into themselves. Later, when the animal dies, as it inevitably will, such people may suffer terrible anguish. I bring this up here because I see it so often. Reading Anitra's book reminded me again of the potential that can be realized through relationship with a cat or any animal. Not stopping at this point—extending that potential to ever wider circles of both people and animals—can allow for a continuous learning that is immensely rewarding.

The Natural Cat is also extremely practical and covers common and mundane problems in a unique way—holistically. That is, the author considers all aspects of the animal's life and environment, both psychological and physical.

I want to emphasize Anitra's sections on declawing and overpopulation. As a veterinarian, I have seen firsthand the incredible suffering of cats who have an amputation of what is to them their fingers. And my work in an SPCA clinic (Society for the Prevention of Cruelty to Animals) brings me face-to-face daily with the suffering and neglect of unwanted animals. It is a blight on our society that such conditions should exist.

I heartily recommend this book to you. Use it as a learning tool and as a source of practical information. May both you and your animal friends profit!

Richard H. Pitcairn, D.V.M., Ph.D.

# Introduction

"You're a what?"

"A cat groomer."

People always think they've misunderstood me when I answer their question, "What do you do for a living?" Then they always want to know how in the world I got to be a cat groomer. It's hard to know where to begin.

When I was a little girl, I had two dreams of what I wanted to be when I grew up. One was to earn my living in the theater. I was so stage-struck that I declared over and over that I would be willing to sweep the floors in a theater if only I were allowed to come even that close to the magic realm.

The other dream was to work with animals. I loved them all, so there again it didn't matter how—as a veterinarian, as a lion tamer, a dog groomer—as long as I could be physically close to animals. I even read about game wardens and forest rangers but decided those jobs wouldn't get me in close enough.

My family considered both of these ambitions to be immature, foolish, and impractical. Nevertheless, against all sober and good advice, I came to New York after I graduated from college and began a career as an actress. I turned out to be one of the lucky ones; I guess you could say I made it. I was never a star and I was never famous, but I did make a nice living in show business, and I enjoyed it to the hilt. I did summer stock and national tours. I sang on Broadway in big hit musicals, made commercials, and appeared on a soap opera.

It was during that time that I got my first cat. Knowing what I do now, I shudder when I think of the dreadful mistakes I made with that cat's feeding—raw kidney, raw liver, and cans of tuna fish. Dear Euryd-ice, she made the best of what she had—me. She took me under her paw and began my training—elementary cat communication and the basics in feline etiquette. She was my beloved companion, my solace in time of trouble. Her beauty was my pride and her humor my joy. When she died, I felt I had lost an irreplaceable part of myself. But one has to go on, and so I did more shows and television commercials, and very soon two more cats moved in to continue my education.

Four years later, while taking a working vacation in Yugoslavia as a yoga instructor for Club Mediterranee, I contracted hepatitis. My illness was long, and recovery was slow. Even when I got back enough strength to work again, I still looked too awful to think of appearing on stage or before a camera. So I started looking for other work. And the job that came my way was working for Dr. Paul Rowan, the well-known cat specialist. One door had closed to me, but another one was opening. I was beginning a second life. It was as if I had been reincarnated without dying in between. My job was mainly to clean. I cleaned the floors, the shelves, the walls. I had to disinfect the arms of the chairs in the waiting room and even the doorknobs. I cleaned the cages or "nooks," as they were called there; food pans; and litter boxes. Working for Dr. Rowan, I learned what *clean* means—a whole new dimension of the word that I never knew existed.

Slowly, as the weeks went by, I became a happy person again. Fate had plunked me in the middle of cat heaven—working for one of the finest veterinarians in the country, exclusively treating cats because he loved them and understood them.

Carole Wilbourn, the feline behaviorist and author of *The Inner Cat*, was then Dr. Rowan's head nurse. She is now his wife. I was always slightly in awe of Carole. Coming out of such a negative time in my own life, I was absolutely mesmerized by her bright, positive attitude about everything. Carole revolutionized many standard practices in veterinary nursing care. One of my professors in college used to say, "The poorest excuse for continuing anything is that it has always been done that way." Well, clinging to the status quo was certainly never one of Carole Wil-bourn's faults. When Carole found that the cats didn't like cold metal cages, the Cat Practice installed mellow wooden ones. Whereas most veterinarians hold cats immobile during examinations and treatment by grasping the scruff of the neck, at the Cat Practice cats were simply dis-tracted with petting and play during the exam.

Persians with matted coats had always been anesthetized and shaved. It was the easiest and fastest way, and no one ever questioned it until Carole Wilbourn asked if there was any way to avoid the anesthetic, because it is so dangerous. She reasoned that, if you have to anesthetize because a shaver hurts, burns, and pulls, why not use scissors to cut the mats out instead? If the cat is nervous and won't stand still, why not send someone into the cat's home where the cat will be more calm and the owner him- or herself can assist? If this is impractical and takes too much time for a busy veterinarian, why not find someone else to do the job?

Carole immediately began a search for the right person to fill the bill, and for reasons that were never clear to me she decided to give me a chance at it. She never asked me if I thought I *could* do it, only if I *wanted* to—automatically eliciting a positive response. Because Carole was such a positive person herself, she had a way of making everyone around her respond positively, too. So, before I was able to voice any reservations, she shoved a little white hat box marked "Grooming Kit" into my hands, along with a ragged piece of tablet paper that had five names and addresses on it. She said that these were my clients and that they were waiting for me to call. Furthermore, she suggested that I use the office phone immediately. Carole was never one to waste time.

Because confidence was not exactly my strong point in those days, I respectfully pointed out to Carole my total ignorance and complete lack of experience in this new field she'd invented. Undaunted, she blithely assured me that, because no one had ever done it before, no one was experienced, and if I just tried it for a while it might work out. Carole always had a wonderful way of making the most revolutionary ideas seem totally logical and simple. I decided the least I could do was give it one heck of a good try.

"Fools rush in"—zap, you're a cat groomer.

When Carole Wilbourn "threw me to the cats," so to speak, the cats caught me. They taught me everything I needed to know from there on in. I *had* to learn from the cats—there was no one else to teach me. I was the slowest student in all Creation at first while I was learning anatomy, skin tensions, fur texture, and scissor angles. The pussycats persevered with me, and I also learned patience and concentration. I watched the cats, I felt the cats, I listened to the cats, and I loved the cats. The love between us opened the doors of communication and the cats gave me lessons in all the things a cat thinks are most important. Cat lessons are there for everybody, you only have to love and ask—not what you want to know but what it is that they would like you to know. First I received cat lessons on how to groom them and how to keep every part of their external bodies just the way they most like it to be.

Because I visited them in their home environment, I was soon made aware of problems and unanswered questions that owners all over New York City had in common. Oh, there were the usual grooming questions about dandruff and shedding, but there were many other questions, too—about random wetting, how to train to the scratching post, runny eyes, and litter box care—things that were outside the realm of grooming.

Of course, my first move was to refer all problems to the veterinarians, assuming that they had all the answers. In this I found I was mistaken. Many of these problems were not in their realm, either. In fact, before long I had collected a whole list of problems that did not seem to be in anybody's realm, so they had all been lumped together under the heading of unsolvable: "There's nothing you can do," "Cats are just like that," and so forth. Well, if there's one thing I learned while working at Dr. Rowan's and observing Carole Wilbourn, it was not to accept such a negative, defeatist attitude. If cats have a problem, physical or mental, or if they are doing something that is destructive either to themselves or their families, there must be some reason other than the fact that "cats are just like that." And once you know the reason for something you're half-way to the solution.

Why won't the cat use the scratching post—or the litter box? *Why* do Persians get mats and dandruff? *Why* is the animal nervous, shy, or aggressive? I looked for the answers. I asked. I read. But in the end it was the cats themselves that came through for me once again. "Stick as close as you can to nature," Dr. Rowan used to say. So I researched how cats handle some of these problems in the wild. If cats are just made that way, I looked to nature to find out why—"What is the purpose of their behavior?" Many answers came from the sick cats and the castoffs—cats so old or sick, so smelly or ugly, that no one wanted them. When I invited them to spend whatever time they had left with me, I never dreamed that they would pay for their keep in the solid gold coin of knowledge gained. You don't learn much from a cat that is young and strong, happy, healthy, and well-adjusted. These castoff cats taught me with their bodies, their patience, and their love. Home care of the sick cat I learned from sick cats. My recommendations concerning proper diet and feeding habits are largely a distillation of what is found in nature. I didn't create any of this information. I only asked the questions, and, by the grace of the cat goddess, the answers came.

So, you see, this book isn't really by me. The information is coming through me but not from me. Knowledge is like the air, it's there for you to use and pass along but not to possess.

New knowledge seems to evolve out of the old. Hopefully this means that the knowledge contained in this book will generate further new knowledge in the mind of each reader. After all, each cat is unique, just as each one of us is unique. I know that with this in mind you will not make the mistake of thinking of anything in this book as "the last word." There is always the possibility of finding an even better way. Perhaps it will be your cat, giving cat lessons to you, who will reveal this even better way. All you have to do is keep your mind open, and love, and ask.

Desirable Behavior in Cats and Owners

Communication and understanding are the two most important links between cats and their owners. It is obvious to sensitive and caring owners that their cats are aware when the owners are unhappy or in ill health. Likewise, the cats respond with joyful play when the owner's mood is jolly.

By understanding the cat's psyche, you are better able to open the pathways to a rewarding and fulfilling relationship—for you and for your feline friend. All you have to do is look at any situation from your cat's point of view.

Communicating with Your Cat

The golden rule for the finicky cat owner is "Don't limit yourself." In your relationship with a pussycat, you will discover new dimensions of sensitivity. When new owners discover petting, they first learn the pleasures of medium and firm stroking. However, there is another dimension of stroking in which you deliberately hold yourself back and touch only the very tips of the hair throughout the entire stroking motion.

The very best lesson in the soft approach can be learned from your cat. First, put your hands behind your back and, bending over, reach out to your cat with just your nose. Then stop, be still, and wait—and your cat will demonstrate to you how very softly it is possible to touch somebody. This approach to a cat—this overture with the nose—demonstrates great trust and friendliness, because you are exposing your eyes and face without having any defense in reserve. It conveys the message "I love you" very nicely. I use it often when greeting a cat client with whom I am already acquainted. However, I never use this approach on a strange cat until I have first ascertained that he or she is fairly calm—although this action does serve to calm a nervous cat.

Another nice dimension in interacting with your cat is throwing a "cat kiss" from across the room. A cat kiss is a long, slow blink with your gaze or attention fixed on the cat's eyes before, during, and after the blink. When throwing a cat kiss, I always think the phrase "I love you" ("I" before, "love" during, and "you" after the blink.)

Cats don't communicate with sound only—in fact, they seldom communicate that way. I notice that cats use the slow eye blink communication when they are feeling relaxed, contented, and secure. I started practicing every time I could get a cat's eye attention and found that I received a return blink from the cat by the third try. Delighted with my break in the language barrier, I began throwing these cat kisses to any and all cats with whom I came in eye contact. I then tried refining my technique. The cats made it clear that screwing up the face during the blink only clouds the issue. The optimum length of time is one or two seconds long, and simplicity is the watchword.

The supreme test came when I began throwing cat kisses to strange felines on the other side of closed windows as I walked down the street. After my technique was perfected, I was thrilled to discover that these strangers would automatically throw back a leisurely reply. They seem to take it in stride that a human walking by would casually throw them a kiss. Only twice have I had the experience of a cat doing a sort of double-take afterward. Looking rather surprised, they seemed to be thinking, "Hey, she speaks Cat!"

Keep in mind that, because cats are so much smaller than we are, they very much enjoy the light touch or the kiss or word thrown from afar. Also remember that cats, being so small, feel very much at our mercy. Often a cat's hiss is a defensive act to try to make the large and threatening human back off just enough so the cat can slip away unharmed. A hissing cat is a frightened cat. Whenever you deal with a cat who is nervous, frightened, or just stand-offish, you must take great pains to be polite—polite in the cat sense.

A really top-notch finicky owner will always be polite with any cat, as a matter of course. Never walk up to cats and scoop them up without first announcing your presence and your intent and asking permission. If you have more than one cat, you can see a demonstration of this sort of politeness by watching a performance of the cats' "I want to sit next to you" ritual. The ritual usually goes like this: Marbles is sleeping on a chair, and Roger jumps up next to her. Roger begins licking the sleeping Marbles, thereby announcing his presence and begging leave to stay. Marbles (1) returns the grooming with a casual lick or two, indicating acceptance; (2) ignores Roger, indicating basic neutrality with "You better not disturb me" undertones; or (3) she can lift her head and growl a rejection, indicating that Roger had better jump down. A cat never just plops down next to another cat. Those tentative licks are our equivalent for saying, "May I?" Impolite cats are simply not acceptable to other cats. Cats are willing to make all sorts of allowances for the humans they love, but isn't it much nicer to slip easily into their society by being polite on their terms?

Controlling Your Cat's Behavior Patterns

One of the cat's greatest fears is fear of the unknown. Conversely, familiarity breeds contentment. Cats love familiar things, patterns, places, and sounds. The very fact that a thing is well known and familiar makes it dear to the cat. We can use this love of sameness as a tool to direct the cat's behavior patterns. If we make certain ground familiar, that is the path the cat will want to take. And to engineer a situation so that the cat wants to do what we want him or her to do is really the only way to even begin controlling a cat's behavior patterns.

You can't train a cat the way you would train a dog or a child. A dog positively enjoys learning to do anything that will please you. And if you're training children you can explain reasons and advantages for behavior patterns you wish them to adopt.

There is, however, one golden rule in all three cases. In training a cat, a dog, or a young child, it is most important that you be consistent. If there is something that you don't want the cat to do, such as jumping on a table when there is food on it, then don't *ever* invite the cat up onto the table. *Never.* Not for any reason. If you see the cat on the table, shove him or her unceremoniously onto the floor with a word of disapproval. You must keep it simple—not confusing.

It is difficult to train a cat not to jump up onto the table and or rifle the wastepaper basket, because they are negative lessons. It is much easier to train the cat *to do* something. For example, if you want a cat *not* to scratch the couch and *to* scratch the scratching post, just forget about the couch, which is the "no-no," and concentrate on building fascinating rituals around the scratching post, which is the "yes-yes." (See the section in Chapter 4, "Reinforcing Use of the Scratching Post.")

Velvet Paws for Human Flesh; Claws for Toys and String

The same principle applies when you're teaching a cat not to use teeth or claws on human flesh or clothing. Don't let anyone play with the cat using their hands or flesh or any part of their own bodies. The cat cannot make the distinction between being allowed to roughhouse with the man of the house and not being allowed to play rough with Great Aunt Ethel when she extends a delicately veined hand to stroke an ear. And heaven forbid you should have young children come to visit who want to hug and kiss a pussycat who has been taught that teeth and claws on human flesh are OK.

My Big Purr was almost a year old when he was left at my door. He had evidently been encouraged to play roughly by someone in his past. About a week after he arrived, we were lying on the floor together and I was stroking him. He was all purrs and stretches. His purrs got louder and louder. Then suddenly, without warning, his body contracted, he trapped my arm in his front claws, pulled my hand into his teeth and pressed his hind claws into the soft flesh of my inner arm, preparing to rake the claws down my skin. I froze; afraid to move.

I didn't know what to do. Purr was not angry at me, he was just so overcome by happiness and love that his emotions overflowed and expressed themselves in this very wild and primitive way. Many cats bite softly to express affection. But Purr's former owner must have made the mistake of having rough play with his hands with Purr, beginning when Purr was still a kitten. This naturally taught Purr that claws on skin were OK. When a cat like that grows up, continuing the pattern, what was amusing in a kitten becomes downright dangerous in a large animal. And Purr at one year old was definitely not small.

Few people know how to break this pattern once they have inadvertently established it. Some begin by hitting the cat, which only reinforces the feeling of roughness and brutality. Some even go so far as to mutilate their pet with a declawing operation. In this case, the cat automatically becomes a biter. In both cases, the situation becomes progressively worse instead of better. The cat adores the owner and reaches out for physical closeness and play in the very way the owner has taught him as a kitten. The cat and the owner both end up sad and lonely. They miss the closeness and fun but don't know how to get it back without the owner getting scratched and the cat getting yelled at.

Of course, the easiest way out is never to start the pattern in the first place. *Never* play with a cat or kitten with your bare hands. Use a toy, a string, or a ball—never your hand (and, incidentally, never use a grooming tool as a toy). In short, if you don't want the cat to scratch something, don't even begin to suggest it. Never let the cat start in the first place.

Use your hands for stroking, petting, grooming, transporting, sometimes medicating, but never for play. To cats, play means teeth and claws—catch and kill. If they are not scratching, pouncing, and biting, it's not play, not really; it's love and cuddle. Show them from the start that hands and skin are for love and cuddle; toys are for play.

If you are dealing with a kitten who gets carried away and carelessly uses claws on the skin, just stop dead and relax toward him and disengage the claws, unhooking them by pushing the feet forward, never pulling. Then immediately put the offending kitten gently but firmly away from you with words of deep disappointment. Do not become excited in any way or raise your voice; you want to put a big damper on all exuberance or emotion. Then ignore the kitten for at least three minutes—don't even allow eye contact. Thus you are demonstrating that claws on skin are socially unacceptable—and cats are very social animals. Do the same thing in exactly the same way every time the kitten uses claws on skin. A kitten learns faster if your reaction does not vary. After five or six calm repetitions of you being disappointed and him being ostracized, the kitten will become very careful not to initiate the undesirable chain of events by being too rough or careless in the first place.

But don't leave a vacuum. Simultaneously, be sure to offer an extra-large amount of acceptable playthings—ball, mouse, strings—to refocus the kitten's attention on acceptable outlets for the catch and kill drive.

When this situation arose with Purr, I was at a loss, completely at his mercy. Purr was no longer a kitten one could calmly unhook and place on the floor. Also, the problem was very strongly established. Obviously it was one more reason why he was put on my doorstep in the first place (besides his spraying problem, because he was unneutered when he arrived.) A big strong cat with weapons like that could easily put a large dog to flight. An inexperienced owner might well be frightened.

It was fortunate that I had enough knowledge to stop Purr's action. By relaxing toward him, I confused him. Prey always pulls away and so, unfortunately, do most people. Press *toward* a cat's teeth and claws, and the cat will stop, totally confused, for a second or two. In those two seconds, then, I had to somehow distract him before he resumed the action. My arm was still encircled in a ring of front claws, my hand clamped to his teeth, the teeth ready to chomp. Those miniature scimitars in the back were denting my soft underarm where he was preparing to rake down.

I didn't know what to do. I had a heartbeat to decide, and I had no answer. No past experience to help me; no bit of forgotten lore bubbling to the surface of consciousness out of all the book learning stored in the depths of my memory. Nothing. My beautiful Purr, my soft and loving friend, was about to injure me and I was helpless. I loved him, and he was hurting me, and my heart was broken. I started to cry.

Purr pulled away! From the look on his face, I knew I had stumbled on an answer. He was so startled he unhooked his claws. So I whimpered and mewed in exaggerated fashion, trying very hard to sound like an injured kitten. Purr looked as if he were dying of embarrassment. Evidently no one had ever gotten through to him before that claws hurt skin. Purr was so upset he didn't know what to do—he couldn't stand to see me cry. Carefully he rolled onto his feet. His ears were sort of sticking out at right angles; his muzzle was all stiff and wrinkling as if he was smelling something that hurt his nose. He moved off, looking so confused and sheepish that I felt almost as bad as when he had me "captured."

I didn't want to change him. But how could I live with this breathtaking animal if he periodically displayed the manners of a cougar? I loved his wildness. But I needed him to learn when to be wild and when to be a velvet-pawed pussycat.

To change an undesirable behavior pattern you have to (1) stop the bad action, (2) distract the cat's attention away from it, and (3) focus attention on a new and desirable action.

After only four or five repetitions of the "crying because of claws" pattern, Purr never again unsheathed a claw to me. However, I do not consider my actions in this case a success. Evidently the old owner had played roughly with Purr while lying on the floor next to him. Lying together on the floor must have triggered the old teeth and claws impulse, and this frightened him for my safety. The last thing he wanted was to see me cry again. So now he always moves away if I try to lie down next to him to pet him. Instead I must be standing or sitting, and he must be perched above or below me—the same level won't do.

I did not successfully fulfill Step 3—focusing his attention on a new and desirable activity. In the tension of that situation, I didn't retain his attention long enough to do it. I shocked and embarrassed him, and now he won't lie next to me on the floor. Today, four years later, I'm still trying to figure out how I should have done it.

The Proper Way to Pick Up a Cat

When I go into someone's home to groom, I always ask the owner to pick up the cat and place him or her on the grooming area. This is because I want to demonstrate to the cat that the beloved, trusted owner approves of the proceedings. I was amazed to see how many owners did not know how to pick up a cat properly. I saw cats dangling by their midriffs, gasping for breath over the owner's arm, and, even more frequently, cats clasped under the armpits with their heavy hindquarters swinging in the air, and their shoulders hunched up to their cheeks with a look of long-suffering patience on their little faces. In such cases, I would always delay the grooming session a moment to give a few pointers on how to pick up the cat comfortably.

There are a few rules to remember before we begin:

1. Before you pick up the cat, announce your intentions of doing so.
2. Before you pick up the cat, *face the cat away from you.*
3. Hindquarters must be supported comfortably. They are the heaviest part of the cat's body.
4. Leave the legs as free as possible to give the cat a feeling of freedom and safety. Cats hate to have their legs or paws held.
5. Don't squeeze or grasp too hard.
6. Never breathe into the cat's ears, eyes, or nose—it tickles.

Once the cat is facing away from you, all you have to do is slip one hand under the cat's chest and the other hand under a thigh or the stomach. In both picking up and putting down, move the forelegs slightly ahead of the hindlegs. When picking him up, this tilts the cat's weight back onto the hand that supports the rear. When putting the cat down, slowly lower him to the floor, slightly headfirst so that he can see where he is going. Because their legs are always left free and pointing toward the floor, the cat feels very safe and secure.

My Big Purr wanted no part of being picked up when I first got him. I had no wish to impose my will on an affectionate and exciting pet but, for the sake of practicality, I knew that I had to be able to pick Purr up to place him in the carrying case for the annual trip to the veterinarian, and there were bound to be other times when I would need to pick him up. So, using cats' love of ritual, I invented a wonderful new game that I call "Pick up/Put down."

Ritual, to *be* ritual, must be repeated frequently. So, for a few weeks, we played Pick up/Put down two or three times a day. I would come up behind Purr, announce my intention by rubbing my thumb against my other fingers, which made a "shushing" sound near his ear, and repeat the ritual phrase "Do you want to come?" His natural reaction was usually to jump up with glee and face me, with an expectant look on his face. I would turn him around to face away from me again, stroke my hands around and underneath his chest and hindquarters, and lift him up a bit, just barely disengaging his feet from the ground. During this action, I always repeated the second ritual phrase, "There's my good boy." The trick is, while cats are learning, you must put their feet back down again before they even begin to get nervous or upset. Design calmness into the pattern, and leave them wanting more. Always follow this ritual with stroking and lavish praise and approval.

For the first few days, the whole procedure took less than ten seconds. By the third day, I was lifting him up about three feet, always keeping him close to my body to help him feel secure. Because I was bent over, I was able to nuzzle my nose and my mouth against his ruff and murmur loving words. The ritual still lasted less than ten seconds. In two weeks, I could lift him up, straighten up myself, and tuck his hindquarters between my arm and body at the side of my waist. His front feet were still left dangling floorward, while my right hand supported his chest—so he still had a feeling of security. I learned from Purr that a cat doesn't wiggle as much if you move about while you're carrying him. So have a definite place to go or a reason for picking him up. If you stand still, keep yourself in control by putting the cat down before he starts wiggling to jump down.

Goodbye for Long or Short Periods

Many of the loving owners I know have wished fervently again and again that they could somehow communicate to their cat the reassurance that they would be back before the day was over. But the owners don't think the cat can understand these things. They say, "He gets so upset when I leave, if only I could make him understand that it's all right—I'll be back soon." Cheer up, you *can* make your cat understand. I had exactly the same thoughts and the same problem. I simply made my leave-taking into a ritual. This dovetailed nicely, incidentally, with my desire to shape Big Purr's behavior along more adventurous lines—he was inclined to experience undue alarm any time he was outside the apartment door.

On a normal working day, when I'm going to be home again to feed the cats dinner sometime before midnight, our ritual is this: I throw my purse and grooming kit into the basket of my three-speed bike and wheel it into position facing the door. Because Purr now knows that he has the leading role in this goodbye ritual, he comes prancing along and leaps up onto the bike seat. "Are you going to walk me to the elevator?" I ask. I always use the same words and say them in the same tone as I lift him up and place him in the bike basket on top of my things. I wait for him to settle himself comfortably, then open the door and wheel him on the bike out of the apartment and down the hall to the elevator, where I park it. Then, while assuring him that he is the most courageous and adventurous cat I have ever met, I pick him up and carry him back to the apartment, giving lots of kisses and nuzzlings and thanking him profusely for his protection. No mugger would dare attack me while Big Purr is on the job. I put him down inside and blink goodbye to all the other cats in sight. Purr sits right inside the door, looking up at me soulfully because he knows that the end of the ritual is coming up. Some days he even reaches up a paw to tap my leg as if asking if we couldn't change the ending this one time and have me stay. It tears my heart but I do have to go out, so I push resolutely on with the usual script. I open the door, step outside, and, right before I close it, I give him a big, strong eye blink—a cat kiss—and say, "See you later, Alligator." One more blink, then I close the door.

If I'm going away for the weekend or off on vacation, the ritual is totally different, and the cats know it. In fact, when the suitcase comes out the first thing Purr does is to leap inside it and refuse to budge in hopes that I'll take him along. It has become very evident to me that my "Goodbye for a long time" ritual is almost superfluous. The suitcase tells them all they need to know. Instead of sitting quietly on the floor, looking up at me soulfully and tapping me politely with his mitten, Purr imposes his body between me and the door, grabs my pants with his claws, and rolls about on his back. He refuses to let go, trying to convince me that now is the time for play. Nevertheless, here again I push on with the prescribed ritual. I disengage Purr and proceed back into the apartment, leaving my suitcase at the door. Instead of the eye blink from afar, I pet and hug each one of the cats, telling them that I love them and will miss them. Then I approach the door again where Purr is waiting. The best way to get Purr not to use claws is to put my face too close to them. So I kneel down and hug him and hum warm air into the short furs on top of his head.

Right before I pick up the suitcase, I use the ritual phrase, "OK, Purr, I'm leaving you in charge." Then I grab the suitcase, slip through the door, throw him a last blink, and lock up.

It is clear from his behavior that he knows full well I'm not coming home that night. Purr, being the dominant male, will communicate this information to the other cats by his attitude when my usual coming-home time rolls around. And anyway, I remind myself as I descend in the elevator, my assistant Louise will be in to feed them. She has her own special games with them that they all enjoy.

Introducing a New Cat in the Home

Every time I'm called on to perform the happy task of introducing a new cat into a single-cat household, I pull out my reference copy of *The Inner Cat,* by Carole Wilbourn, and reread Chapter 3, "Introducing New Feline Members into the Household." (*The Inner Cat* is a definitive work on feline behavior and goes at the top of my recommended reading list.) Follow very carefully her ten basic steps, giving special attention to keeping your own attitude very casual and controlling your impulse to touch or even look at the new cat for a few days. I have found that this is really a fool-proof method. As in any situation where you hope to elicit a particular behavioral response from your cat, these ten steps simply structure the situation so that the response you hope for is the easiest and most natural one for the cat to adopt. Here, straight from *The Inner Cat,* are the ten steps:

1. *Have a neutral party bring in the newcomer.* If the party is someone your cat is very fond of, he may feel slighted.

2. It's preferable for the newcomer to be in a cat carrier with a wire top so that your cat can observe him. The carrier should be lined with strips of newspaper in case the newcomer has an accident.

3. Some of the strips of newspaper (if clean) can be discreetly placed on the floor where your cat will find them. From them he'll be able to get a good whiff of the newcomer until he decides to go closer to the carrier.

4. You should be oblivious to the new arrival even if he's staring you right in the face. This would be a good time to join your guest in some light refreshment to preoccupy your mind with eating.

5. Don't discuss how your cat's going to react. Talk about anything that will get your mind off the encounter. A light, cheerful subject is best.

6. When your cat's good and ready, he'll strut over to inspect the newcomer. Don't be surprised if he's sniffing and hissing at the same time. Breathe deeply and concentrate on your juicy conversation. You don't want to pass your nervousness on to your cat.

7. Don't offer your cat any words of encouragement. If you interfere, your cat will react negatively. It must be his decision.

8. The newcomer should remain in the carrier for at least two hours. This way your cat will feel he has the upper hand.

9. After the two hours, lure your cat away from the carrier with food or catnip. While you're distracting him, your friend can unfasten the carrier so that your cat won't feel you're responsible when the newcomer pops out.

10. Don't be surprised if there are inflated tails, hissing, and even puffed-up bodies. In case of a bad skirmish, a spray of water will

cool things out. You can't expect the relationship to be an instant success. If your cat should simply decide he's going to ignore the newcomer by retreating to another room the moment after the arrival, casually drop some of the newspaper from the newcomer's carrier in the room with your cat. If he still insists on being alone, when the two hours are up have your friend open the carrier and the newcomer will take it from there. Don't try to sneak in pats with the newcomer. Your cat will only have to smell your hands to know you've deceived him.

Carole also suggests that you give your cat a lot of extra attention for a week or so before the new cat arrives. Give him extra eye and voice contact as well as petting. Make your cat feel really secure, so that it won't enter his mind that the newcomer may have come to replace him.

I have found, in Step 2, that if the party bringing the new cat holds the carrier on his or her lap for twenty minutes or so it establishes with great clarity the connection between the new cat and the stranger, as opposed to any connection with the owners. If I am the person bringing the new cat, I wear some perfume and pet the new cat with my perfume-scented palms, further establishing a scent relationship between the new cat and me. I've found that Step 5 is the one that I most often have to remind nervous prospective owners of. It's such a temptation to watch the cats. Have three or four subjects ready that will take the new owners' attention off the drama taking place in the middle of the living room.

Dangers in the Home

Cats who belong to a loving owner just naturally assume that the owner will never hurt them. They will stick their noses into the oven, not realizing you are about to light it; they will leave their tails trailing about in the door, not realizing you are about to slam it. Our beloved pets are not frightened, and so they are not cautious. If we try a little bit to think like a cat, we have a better chance of protecting them.

For us, the sense of sight is Number One; to a cat, *smell* is much more important. Think of the times that you have seen a cat looking in the mirror at himself. You probably wondered why he seemed disinterested. Didn't his eyes tell him that another cat was there? Yes, they *did*. But his nose told him that he was alone, and his nose is what he believed.

Cats go places that we wouldn't think of going because their noses tell them these are nice places—they're interesting and smell delicious. Cats have been locked in refrigerators because the owner turns away and, without looking, slams the door closed. The owner would never think of crawling into a refrigerator, so it does not occur to him or her that a cat might find it fascinating. Insulation muffles the cat's cries, and by the time the cat is missed it is often too late. With a cat loose in the house, you can never again open or close any door or drawer with automatic mindlessness. For the rest of your life with a cat, you must always *look as you close*.

We all tend to forget that for cats the home is not a natural environment. We have taken the cats out of their natural environment for our own pleasure, so it behooves us to protect them from dangers that they do not automatically recognize as such. Most cats are curious. Don't ever leave your window or the door to the balcony open; the scents that blow in are absolutely fascinating. Almost all cats find cooking odors from other homes and body odors from other people's animals and birds positively irresistible. Sooner or later your cat will explore them. Chances are he will explore them repeatedly day after day, going back again and again to the open window or balcony. Sooner or later there will be a little stray piece of fluff blowing by or a tiny insect on the wing that will capture his attention completely for the moment. As he lunges to capture that elusive object, one second is all it takes for him to fall. I have come to dread the springtime in New York City because it ushers in the season of death and mutilation from falls. Dr. Leo Camuti, the famous cat specialist, now eighty-five years old, has said that of all the different cases he sees in New York, the most frequent are cats falling out of windows and off balconies.

In all my years as a cat groomer in New York, I have observed that all the cats who fall have one thing in common—each one is a cat to whom "it could not possibly happen." This group of cats is divided into two categories—either "He's been sitting there for eight years, he's certainly not going to fall out now" or "She's terrified of the balcony—how is she going to fall if she never goes out there?" These cats are crippled or die because they are not protected. The cats who are likely to fall out, the ones who are lively, who would obviously leap to the rail of the balcony if allowed to do so, are the ones who are protected because their danger is obvious. So they never fall.

I have twice heard of cats falling from a window that was open "only an inch." In one of these cases, I know for a fact that the owner spoke the truth—but if cats want to explore the outside world they begin by thrusting their noses through even the smallest opening. They work and pry until the whole head gets through. Then pressing their shoulders under is easiest of all, and there they are—trapped on a narrow ledge.

Females in heat are especially prone to this maneuver. They know that there is no male inside the apartment or home, and if they get the merest whiff from one outdoors it's all over. And declawed cats, of course, have notoriously poor balance.

Even if you could swear that your cats are fully aware of the dangerous distance between the ledge and the street, you must remember that pussycats' minds are different from ours. They do not automatically assume that that distance is always going to be that way. Sure, you held Samantha up to the railing, and she looked over, and she was scared. But that doesn't mean that tomorrow she won't forget and assume that the floor height on this side of the railing must be the same on the other side too.

Cats perceive the world differently from the way we do. They live almost exclusively in the present, with a very limited and hazy memory of the past and almost no concept of the future. Their concept of space and depth differs from ours, too. Remember also that cats frequently fall out of windows that are open from the top. Window screens are not expensive.

Once you've screened the windows, the average home is still booby-trapped with objects harmful to a pussycat. For example, many simple cleaning compounds such as Lysol, as well as dish-washing compounds, are fatal if the cat gets even one lick of them. I wash the litter box with plain cleanser (such as Bon Ami or Comet) or Ivory Liquid, and then I rinse it to a fare-thee-well because anything cats step in is going to go into their mouths. Cats are always licking their paws, especially if they smell something disagreeable on them. So think twice about anything you use to clean any surface in the home. Any product containing phenol is particularly deadly. If I use any compound about which I am in doubt, and I must admit I'm in doubt about most of them, I just rinse like crazy. Of course, you must store any cleaning fluids or medicines in a safe cat-proof place.

The fumes from moth balls destroy the cat's liver cells. A cat accidently locked in a closet (or sleeping by choice in a closet) where moth crystals or balls are used can inhale enough fumes in a few hours to destroy the liver beyond repair. Such cats with irreversible liver damage are usually put to sleep by the veterinarian rather than allowing them to endure a slow, lingering death. If you're going to use moth crystals, make sure the garments and their crystals are in a tightly locked air-tight container, preferably inaccessible to the cat.

You should never have occasion to use mouse and rat poisons—for obvious reasons. But city people, like it or not, must be prepared to face the cockroach problem. Roach sprays and powders are deadly to small animals and extremely debilitating and dangerous to us big ones. My own alternative is roach traps. Although I have found their effectiveness to be far below satisfactory when used as directed, I have added a refinement of my own that renders them diabolically successful. Every morning and every evening when I feed the cats, I simply take a tiny dot of cat food and place it in the middle of a sticky roach trap. The roaches can't resist it. This trap baiting must be done twice a day, and I find it's best to use only one trap at a time so as not to confuse the little horrors.

A staggering number of plants are poisonous. Poinsettias head the list, with azaleas and dieffenbachia running a close second. Here is a list of some others: philodendron, ivy, chrysanthemums, mistletoe berries, rhubarb leaves, cherry (fruit, bark, stones, and leaves), iris leaves and roots, most bulbs (such as daffodil, jonquil, narcissus, and Star of Bethlehem), poison ivy, privet, oak (acorns, shoots, and leaves), mushrooms, oleander; sumac, sweet pea, and rosary pea (seeds and pods), uncooked potatoes (eye and sprouts), and apricot and peach pits. Even if you decide to play it safe and have only hanging plants of the most innocent variety, there are still plant-related dangers at Christmastime. Angel hair cuts and can be lethal if swallowed or if a tiny piece is inhaled into the cat's lungs. Tinsel is just as dangerous as any string or rubber band. But most dangerous of all is the water that the Christmas tree stands in. The piney fragrance may invite your cats to drink but if they do they could die from it. So be sure to cover the Christmas tree stand in such a way that even the most determined pussycats could never get their tongues into the water.

Many commonly used cat toys are quite dangerous. Strings, yarn, and rubber bands have caused many cat deaths. Cat's tongues are constructed so that it is almost impossible for them to spit anything out. The stereotyped picture of kittens playing with a ball of yarn can easily become a horror story. Once they start to swallow a string, they can't stop—they can only swallow more. Strangulation can occur from yarns and string. Rubber bands can become wrapped around the intestine.

Surgery can sometimes save such an animal, but all too often the tangle is too complex to undo before the pet expires. By all means let your cat chase string, play with yarn—but *never, never* without supervision.

It's the same with tin-foil balls, corks, and cellophane balls. These articles make stimulating cat toys that crackle and skitter across the floor, tempting even the most lethargic of overweight felines to have a go at the game. But when play time is over, store such toys in an inaccessible container. A piece of cork can cause choking; a piece of aluminum foil is not digestible and can block the intestine. Cellophane cigarette wrappers turn "glassy" when they come into contact with the digestive juices in the cat's stomach. Death by internal hemorrhage follows cuts from such cellophane.

Many toys sold in pet shops and supermarkets are actually quite dangerous because the decorations and trim are only glued on, and when they fall off they are easily swallowed by the cat. Choose toys that are crocheted or sewn together. Don't allow the cat to play with any object that could possibly be swallowed—to be on the safe side nothing smaller than a ping-pong ball. Incidentally, a ping-pong ball makes a great cat toy and an absolutely safe one. Another winner is the cardboard tube from inside the toilet paper or the cardboard strip from a coathanger.

The Tree House Animal Foundation hits the nail on the head with their slogan, "Remember, your cat cannot judge safety for himself, he needs your help."

Game Time and Encouraging Exercise

Now that you're thinking like a cat to keep your cat safe, let's think like a cat to encourage exercise and have some fun. All cats need exercise. If your cats do not seem to exercise much, you'll have to figure out ways to make them want to do so without letting them know that you want them to. The secret is to structure situations that will tempt them to chase or jump or run. Cats are very imaginative and creative. When they play with a piece of paper or a ball, they really make themselves believe that that thing is some living creature that they are actually going to catch and kill. They endow that toy with all sorts of wonderful qualities such as juiciness, delectable smell, and wilyness; they unsheathe their claws, slash with their fangs, growl, and sometimes even salivate. It therefore behooves us, their partners in play, if we wish to come up to their highly imaginative standards, to throw ourselves enthusiastically into the role of the startled, fluttering bird, the terrified chipmunk, or the innocent, tender fieldmouse.

There is one time in nature when activity is a necessity—before meals. If cats living in the wild are going to eat, they must first "catch and kill." Because cats love ritual, a good before-meal ritual could involve a "catch and kill" game.

What should you use to tempt them? Different cats have different tastes in toys. What frightens one cat will fascinate another. There are several elements to consider: size, weight, texture, sound, and smell. An interesting crinkly sound or a scratchy scrapy sound when something is dragged across the floor is fascinating to a cat. Crumpled paper thrown across a bare floor or a tissue or wax paper ball might do the trick, because cats usually prefer lightweight toys. Just remember—things a cat catches and kills in the wild are all lightweight. Have you ever held a bird or a mouse? They weigh practically nothing.

Texture is another interesting aspect to consider. Cats are much more aware of texture than we are. Big Purr's favorite toy, which he brings to me to have me throw for him, is a large-size pipe cleaner twisted into the outline of a butterfly. This particular kind of pipe cleaner has little sharp prickly things twisted into the usual chenille. I should think they would prick his sensitive lips and nose, but I've tried other pipe cleaners and he always goes looking for his old favorite, the dirty old prickly one.

If you want the cat to chase a ball or string or pipe cleaner, you're going to have to do your best to make the toy behave as much like "prey" as possible. For example, don't throw the ball *to* the cat—the mouse doesn't run into the cat's arms. The mouse runs *away* from the cat or scampers innocently by where the cat lies crouched and waiting. Draw the string *across* in front of the cat, preferably almost out of reach, and make the motion jumpy and erratic, like a living creature scurrying along unaware of the fierce and lurking predator. Throw the ball from *behind* the cat so that it rolls past him or her and away like a little creature who has been alarmed and is streaking for its hole.

When Purr and I play with his pipe cleaner, I throw it up in an arc in front of him so that the apex is three or four feet above the ground. His part is to take one or two steps and then leap, capturing the helpless pipe cleaner in mid-air. Obviously the pipe cleaner is a little bird who has been frightened by Purr's presence—and I assume that I'm the bush where the bird has been sitting. He also has a variation where, instead of "capturing" it, he bats it viciously into the bedroom, runs after it, and pounces. I always wish at these times that a photographer were standing by to capture forever that lithe body stretched out in mid-air, head back, fangs bared, and the look of fierce concentration in the eyes. He looks so ferocious and becomes so emotionally involved in the game that I'm sure he salivates, preparatory to eating what he catches. For that reason, I try not to play this game except before meals. After each catch, I always praise him effusively. It took me longer to learn how to throw the pipe cleaners correctly than it took Purr to learn to catch them. He was a natural—I wasn't.

Success is an important part of game playing. Remember that a game, to be a game, must be fun—and failure is no fun. So don't roll the ball so fast that the scurrying creature that it represents makes it safely to its hole every time. Your cat will soon begin to feel that it's hopeless to try and will just give up. Instead, endow the fieldmouse with a thorn in its toe so that it cannot scurry fast enough to escape the fierce predator. Make the winging bird a fledgling whose little feathers cannot lift it far enough to escape your cat's sharp claws. Then, when your cat achieves success, enjoy it with him. Express delight, give praise, and pet him.

Even though Purr is a large cat, he prefers his ultralightweight, small, delicate toy. Once a month or so I dip it in catnip powder to add the dimension of smell and taste. He enjoys that a lot, too.

Little Karunaji, who is a half-grown kitten, doesn't care a rap for Purr's favorite toy. Karunaji stole the metal replica of the Eiffel Tower with a tiny thermometer set into it that sits on my bedroom windowsill. Because it is three inches long and solid brass, it appears too large and heavy for a cat's taste. The texture of cold metal would seem unappealing to a cat. But Karunaji loves it. It makes a satisfying clatter when she bats it across the bare floorboards. Karunaji also loves a long, heavy seashell and a clattery walnut shell.

A crumpled-up paper tied to the end of a long string is very hard to resist. Many cats respond better to something that seems to leap up—for example, something tied to a string can be made to leap up suddenly. A Toughie Mouse from the Felix Katnip Tree Company (which can be ordered by mail) is smaller and heavier, while a sheet of tablet paper crumbled into a ball is larger and lighter, with the added advantage of going "klittery-scrape" as you drag it along the floor. The following are all supersuccessful toys: peacock feather, ping-pong ball, Super Ball, pipe cleaner, seashell, walnut shell, green bean, toilet paper cylinder.

I divide cats into two categories—the mousers and the bird catchers. The mousers love to chase things along the floor and pounce on them; the bird catchers like my Big Purr execute breathtaking leaps into the air to trap flying pipe cleaners.

There is a great advantage to having a favorite game in which the *same* toy is always used in pretty much the *same* way, in the *same* area of the home, and always at the *same* time of day, because this sameness constitutes a ritual—and you know how cats love rituals. When you go away, this ritual can easily be taught to the cat sitter and will make the sitter seem more like a member of the family to your cat.

Catnip is a powerful tool that can be used for positive reinforcement. Catnip is a stimulant—a mild aphrodisiac. When powdered, it has a snufflike effect that elicits a good sneeze. And it's just a heck of a lot of fun. Owners really should keep a supply on hand. My cats' favorite brand is Peppy Powder Kitty Snuff, which I get from the Felix Katnip Tree Company.

One word of advice: You must keep control of the catnip source—keep it in a screw-top jar, because cats will open things you thought they couldn't open and will go places you thought they couldn't get to in order to get at the catnip. One day you'll come home to find your cats rolling drunkenly on the rug, catnip littered all about. I'm not saying there is anything really wrong with this—the catnip won't hurt them. One good binge a year will brighten any cat's life. But cats become immune to the effect of catnip if it is used too frequently.

Dr. Rowan, the cat specialist for whom I worked, used to give catnip to every cat on the examining table. He used Peppy Powder Kitty Snuff, too. It was a wonderful way to distract the cats and help them to enjoy his gentle and thorough examination. Then he'd also throw a little catnip into the cat's carrying case so that the whole experience of going to the veterinarian, being examined, and getting a shot was sort of enveloped in a heavenly cloud of catnip. Out of the whole experience, that fabulous catnip is what the cats remembered—especially those cats whose owners never bothered to have catnip at home. Boy, did they love going to see Dr. Rowan!

The office cats, however, were quite another story. There were always two or three of these cats in residence running around. They were strays found injured in the street, cats whose owners brought them in and then deserted them, or cats with terminal illnesses being kept alive with carefully regulated doses of powerful medication because they were not suffering and they had indicated that they didn't want to pass on yet. They worked their way—acting as hostesses and nurse's aides, calming the patients and their owners. These office cats were constantly exposed to catnip. It was wafted in the air, bits and pieces fell to the floor several times a day—they could have it whenever they chose. I was surprised to learn soon after I started to work there that of all the resident cats there wasn't one who cared a rap about catnip. They were overexposed. That really saddened me—all the others were having such a lot of fun. So ever since then I've always been very careful not to give my cats catnip in any form except once every two weeks. Then we have a party. I put both Felix Katnip Trees (scratching posts) over on their sides and sprinkle them with catnip. I also sprinkle catnip on the floor around the posts. All my cats sniff and sneeze, roll and rub, lick and growl, and thrash around to their hearts' content. After an hour, I vacuum the whole mess up because by that time the entire group is stretched out sleeping the sleep of the sated. What a bash! Of course, when I'm going away I make sure that they have not had a catnip party for at least two weeks before I leave so that that happy ritual can then be performed by the sitter.

Diet

Diet is a tool that any pet owner can use to build health, long life, resistance to disease, and a joyous and even temperament. It is a tool so powerful that it is almost a magic wand. *What* you feed your cats and, of equal importance, *when* you feed them is something you, the owner, and no one else, can control. The magic wand is yours alone.

When I started grooming, I was still working part time for Dr. Paul Rowan. I realized that I had a unique opportunity to reinforce details of home care, because I was spending a full hour with each owner during the grooming session. So I asked Dr. Rowan if there was any information that he wanted me to pass along during the groomings. He thought for a split second and replied that I should try to get all the owners to remove food between meals and to have them add yeast and wheat germ to the food. He explained that removing the leftover food after a half hour or so is more like the natural state, because wild animals don't smell food and nibble all day long. And, he said, the added yeast and wheat germ would raise the protein quality of the whole meal and keep the cat's resistance to disease high. So I dutifully passed these two bits of information along to every client I saw.

When I returned again the next month for the usual grooming session, I found that these two simple dietary changes had caused startling improvements in the cats' coats. In fact, the changes were incredible. Persians who always had some matting now had almost none. Oily coats were less oily. Dull, harsh coats began to feel soft and look fluffier and brighter. Of course, I should have expected these results: "You are what you eat." It only makes sense that better-quality food will result in better overall health and therefore a better quality of fur. It's obvious now, as I look back. But at that time it was a big bonus. That was the beginning.

Then I began to notice that cats whose health was below par did not show the change in coat quality as dramatically. Therefore, because coat quality seems to be a barometer of the internal health of the cat, I began nutritional research into helping the cat's body overcome various physical ailments. I had seen the promise in those improved coats, so I knew that if I could upgrade the cat's general health the shiny, plushy coat would just naturally follow, like the reward for a job well done. Eight years and several hundred cats later, I can say that I was right.

The Primary Feeding Rule: Remove Food Between Meals

Dr. Rowan's advice, "Stick as close as you can to nature; that way you can never go too far wrong," has helped me out many a time. Let us examine how Mother Nature takes care of her children and arranges to keep them happy, healthy, and strong.

Cats in the wild eat once a day—*if* they are young and strong and lucky. For a wild cat, being served food twice a day would be a luxury bordering on decadence. In the wild, times of fast occur naturally because of scarcity of game, inclement weather, or because the animal is feeling sick. A day or two or even a week may go by without the taking of a meal. Nature provides these fasting times for a very good reason. During a fast, the blood and energy that are used for digestion and assimilation are available for use in other areas. Healing and repair are accelerated during a fast. Waste disposal becomes more complete, and the body is able to deep-clean itself. A backup of wastes in the system putrifies— and germs breed in putrifaction. So Mother Nature keeps her children free from disease by providing periodic fasts during which the intestines, urinary tract, lungs, and the pores of the skin can get a good housecleaning. The short fast we provide for our animals between their two regular meals a day is little enough time to give the body so it can process the food eaten and accomplish the necessary waste disposal.

There is also a second reason for removing food between meals. It is the *smell* of food (not the taste) that triggers the brain to prepare the body for digestion. When food is smelled, the whole metabolism is slowed so the body can concentrate on digesting the food. Blood flow and waste disposal are affected, and all the organs except the stomach are undersupplied with blood during this process. If the cats are constantly smelling food, the trigger mechanism in their brains that starts the whole digestive process will soon wear out and fail to respond. Even the odor from a dirty food bowl can cause the trigger mechanism to keep the cat's body in constant preparation for digesting food. Because of the resultant under-supply of blood to the organs, such cats age faster than those whose food area is kept scrupulously clean.

Leaving food available all day is also the primary cause of the finicky eater syndrome. The slowed metabolism is a cause of several health problems—among them dandruff, obesity, and skinniness. If a cat has a poor appetite, the answer is not to leave more food available for longer periods but just the opposite—withhold food for a meal or two to give that trigger response a chance to rest.

You will be in harmony with nature's rhythms if you remember that your domestic cat's food equals the wild cat's mouse. The mice do not lounge around all day under the cat's nose waiting to be eaten. Meals are an important, but separate, part of the animal's day.

By all means, feed your cats twice a day—morning and evening. But be sure to leave the food available for only one-half hour—certainly no longer than forty-five minutes. Then remove it and wash everything nice and clean so that no smell remains. Leave fresh water for them to drink at all times.

Special treats of food are fun and can also be useful for hiding medica-tion or for reinforcing a desirable behavior pattern. The best time to offer a treat is about fifteen minutes after the regular meal, as if, on their way back to the lair, your cats had chanced on an unwary mouse. But cer-tainly treats should not be a daily habit—otherwise, they are no longer treats but become old hat.

The No-No's: Foods to Avoid

Early in my search for a high-quality food—one with a minimum of pre-servatives, colorings, and other nonfood ingredients—it became obvious to me that most cat food stocked on grocery shelves did not seem to have the primary purpose of building health. Most simply sustains life, at least for a moderate amount of time, before it endangers the cat's health with chemical additives, imbalances, and/or general low quality.

Ingredients such as tuna and artificial flavors and scents tend to attract the cats and "hook" them. Artificial colors are there to attract the owners (cats are color blind—they see only black, white, and red). Artificial flavors and colors are not food but chemicals that undermine health.

In researching the foods available, I was surprised to find that the manufacturers of every single cat food available in the grocery store could produce the results of one or more scientific tests proving beyond all doubt that their food was absolutely wonderful—the very best. Also, I viewed an "unbiased" report on pet foods on the television news, and it too stated in effect that everything on the shelf was perfectly fine because government regulations were very strict.

Evidently my standards are quite a bit different from those of the government. Preservatives such as BHA, BHT, colorings, artificial flavorings, and scents are chemicals that, in sufficient amount, are deadly poisons. In lesser amounts, they produce illness—but in really minute quantities any damage done builds up so slowly that it is hard to measure. Therefore these smaller amounts have been declared "safe." My feeling is simply that if you do not have to include these nonfood chemical substances in a diet at all, that is by far the safest choice. If a substance in a package marked "cat food" can be considered harmful in any way—in whatever quantity—I avoid that cat food completely. In some cases, research has not succeeded in discovering whether or not the body can successfully dispose of these chemicals with the other wastes or if the body retains them so that they build up over the months and years. Furthermore, scant research has been done on the danger encountered when different chemicals, some from one product and some from another, combine within the cat's body. I won't take a chance. I prefer absolute safety and only the highest-quality nutrition.

Dry Cat Food

Dry food is high in ash and is a prime suspect in causing cystitis and bladder stones. The protein quality in dry food is low. Dry cat food causes the urine to be *alkaline* because of the low quality of the protein, while a cat fed on high-quality protein tends to have an *acidic* urine. An acidic urine prevents the growth of cystitis germs and helps dissolve stones. So, besides being a possible *cause* of cystitis and stones because of its ash content, dry food also *promotes* optimum conditions for the growth of these germs by virtue of the lower urine acidity.

One brand of dry cat food carries the slogan "Lowest in ash of all dry foods." A clever piece of advertising: It is perfectly true. However, this is like saying that grapefruit is the lowest in acid of all citrus fruits. This statement is also perfectly true, but grapefruit, after all, is still a citrus and is still acidic—just as all dry food is still higher in ash than other foods.

All the veterinarians I've worked with caution against dry food and expressly forbid it once cystitis has been diagnosed. Conversely, dry food manufacturers can produce test results proving that a connection between dry food and cystitis is, if not actually nonexistent, then, at least inconclusive. I won't take a chance.

Acceptable Crunchies

If you would like to feed your cat crunchies and be sure that all the side effects will be beneficial, try two or three yeast tablets or one desiccated liver tablet.

Dry food does not clean the teeth, it never has and it never will. No one claims that—not even the dry food manufacturers. I have met numerous cats formerly on an all dry food diet with the worst tartar in the world. To help clean teeth, Dr. Rowan recommends broiled chicken neck vertebrae. The vertebrae are the *only* cooked poultry bones that are allowed, because they do not splinter, they crumble. Do not feed any other cooked poultry bone to your cat except the neck vertebrae. This, like all meat, must be cooked because of the danger of parasites. No matter how expensive the meat, don't take a chance. Some of those parasites are incurable and fatal when they reach the lung or heart. Most cats prefer their chicken neck broiled or roasted as opposed to boiled in water. I suggest presenting the first serving in the bathroom on the tiles, or better yet, in the tub, because the vast majority of cats become extremely excited on sniffing the poultry and tend to revert to primitive behavior—drooling, growling, and muttering, dragging the piece away from the rest of the group even if there is no group present, pretending to kill it over and over again. It's fun to watch, and you may see a side of your cat that hasn't come out before.

One word of caution: too much chicken neck tends to make the stool hard, so I never give an entire meal of neck vertebrae. Give one or two vertebrae as dessert after a half of a normal meal to which you have added an extra half-teaspoonful of bran and a teaspoonful of water. This will condition the stool and overcome the hardening effects of the chicken neck. Give only one to three vertebrae per cat once or twice a week.

Semimoist Food in Packets

Almost every brand of semimoist cat food can be said to be "complete nutrition." That's all well and good, but what else is contained in that convenient little package of "complete nutrition"? If a manufacturer wants to make a lot of money on a food product for human or animal consumption, the first criterion is to make something with the longest possible shelf life. The longer a food can be stored, the larger the potential profit will be.

The amount of preservatives used in semimoist food is so great that such food's shelf life approaches infinity. I have a fantasy that some day in the future—let's say, 10,000 years from now—an archeological expedition from another galaxy will land on the planet Earth. Amidst the rubble, the rust, and the cinders, they will unearth in various places these intriguing little packets filled with colorful little morsels as tender, moist, and juicy as the day they were manufactured. Thinking they have come on some article of human cuisine, they will set to work analyzing several examples of these tidbits and, discovering the amount of artificial color, artificial flavor, artificial scent, and preservatives (sometimes up to three) contained in these morsels, those scientists from space will look at each other, shake their heads sadly, and probably remark, "Tsk, tsk, no wonder the race died out."

If you still have any doubt as to why I would not use semimoist food, I suggest you look at the stool from a cat or dog fed on these substances. The stool looks like technicolor plastic.

Tuna and Other Fish

Even before the dry food and semimoist food, there was tuna fish. "Tuna junkie" is a phrase used by veterinarians to describe a cat "hooked" on tuna. The flavor is so strong that cats who eat a lot of tuna come to believe that tuna is the only thing that constitutes food—nothing else fits into that category for them. Tuna is used as an ingredient in a large majority of canned cat foods precisely because of this strong addictive flavor.

Canned tuna fish in the cat's diet has two drawbacks. First, it tends to rob the cat's body of vitamin E. When the stored vitamin E is sufficiently depleted, a condition called *steatitis* results. Steatitis causes the cat first to become extremely nervous and then to become supersensitive in all the nerve endings in the skin. It is very painful for such cats to be touched in any way. If an autopsy is done on such a cat, the fat is buttercup yellow instead of being white. The disease can be cured by giving megadoses of vitamin E carefully supervised by a veterinarian and, of course, by discontinuing any food that will deplete the body's stores of that nutrient.

On mentioning to one veterinarian that I had noticed some cat food companies were adding vitamin E to the tuna fish, the doctor replied that its effectiveness would be like putting a little cobalt therapy into a pack of cigarettes. Besides destroying vitamin E, tuna fish contains insoluble mineral salts that can form stones and gravel in the bladder and urinary tract. All fish contain these salts, but tuna has the highest concentration.

Ham and Pork

Ham and pork contain fat globules so large that they clog the cat's blood vessels. Just think of your own tiniest capillary and then think what those globules must do in the capillaries and veins of a cat fifteen times smaller than yourself. The preservatives and colorings used in bacon, hot dogs, sausages, and lunch meats are, frankly, lethal in sufficient quantity—even for us big animals. Also, I don't believe in polluting a cat's system with the nitrates and nitrites that are used to preserve most of these meats.

The High-Quality Diet: Fluff City in Thirty Days

Canned foods, although not the best choice, are a nice, easy, middle-of-the-road diet. Recently two new foods have come on the market that seem superior to anything we've had available before—Foods of Nature and Cornucopia—because they are made without by-products or preservatives. If you pick up any canned cat food in your supermarket and read the minute printing under the heading "Ingredients," you will undoubtedly see the words "Meat by-products" or "Beef by-products." The term *by-products* does *not* refer to intestines, eyes, veins, bones, and so on. Those things can be classified as meat—they are part of the animal and can be made into hot dogs and such. "By-products," on the other hand, are glandular wastes; secretions high in hormones and therefore considered too dangerous to be used in human food.

Surprisingly, the price of Foods of Nature and Cornucopia is just slightly *less* per ounce than the usual canned foods (perhaps because they don't do the advertising and marketing that the major cat and dog food companies do). I prefer Foods of Nature beef, chicken, liver, and kidney or Cornucopia Super Stars, which I buy by the case from a wholesale pet food distributor. Be sure that you don't buy the fish flavor. Also, be sure that organ meat constitutes no more than one-sixth of the weekly diet because, if a cat killed an animal in the wild for dinner, only one-sixth of the prey would be organs. If you can't find either of these brands in your area (check with both pet food suppliers and health food stores), buy a canned food with no fish and not too much organ meat—Friskies Mixed Grill or Beef and Liver or Kal Kan Poultry Dinner or Bits O'Beef. Because these products contain preservatives and by-products, I advise adding egg and table scraps to try to make the amount of food more and the percentage of preservatives and by-products less. Baby food meat and vegetable mixes such as Junior High Meat Dinner are much better. You could use it once or five or six times a week, adding Vita-Mineral Mix as described later.

No canned food is perfect, because every canned food is processed by heat, and many vitamins are destroyed by heat. Cats who hunt and kill in the wild consume the whole mouse, right down to the whiskers. They will eat some hair and probably get a litle dirt off the ground in the process. Nature has a purpose in letting the cat ingest these little extras that are not present in our nice, clean cans of food. Hair is roughage, minerals, and protein. Dust is full of minerals. The contents of the mouse's stomach is predigested grain full of B vitamins and enzymes. And the mouse was alive a moment before. The meat is still pulsing with life (I wonder how long the meat inside of that can has been dead). How shall we supply the missing elements? Let's think of building a mouse!

To supply the contents of the mouse's stomach, we will use wheat germ and bran. To supply the minerals and roughage of the mouse's hair, we will use bran, again, and kelp. To supply something living, something still alive when your cat eats it: yeast. The yeast will also raise the quality of the protein in the entire meal and, along with the wheat germ, will replace those B vitamins that were destroyed by heat during the processing of the can.

I add lecithin granules because they emulsify fatty wastes. They help do away with dandruff and make the coat texture absolutely gorgeous. For long-haired cats, lecithin granules are a must. Because cats' requirements for vitamin E are very high and because vitamin E in food is extremely perishable, I keep a bottle of 100-unit vitamin E capsules available in the refrigerator. Three times a week, I snip off the end of one and squeeze a drop onto my finger and then wipe it off on the cat's eye tooth so he or she will lick it off. I also add about a quarter teaspoonful of cod liver oil to the food three times a week to supply vitamins A and D.

At first you may think that you need a full-fledged chemist or a master chef to implement the plan. Take heart. In working with hundreds of very busy New Yorkers, I soon realized that if I wanted all of my cat friends to have the very best it was absolutely necessary to devise a way that was fast and simple for the owners.

Here's what I came up with:

VITA-MINERAL MIX

1½ cups yeast powder (any food yeast, brewer's, tarula, or flaked)

½ cup kelp powder or granules

1 cup lecithin granules

1 cup wheat germ, toasted (raw wheat germ goes rancid even if refrigerated and rancid wheat germ is toxic)

1 cup bran

½ cup dolomite or bone meal

- Mix together and store in a covered coffee can or similar container. Be sure to *refrigerate* (everything but the lecithin and kelp perishes very quickly at room temperature).

- Add 3 teaspoonsful of Vita-Mineral Mix to each large 14-oz. can of cat food. Use 2 teaspoonsful of Mix for small 6½-oz. cans and 1 teaspoonful per jar of baby food.

- Three times a week, give one drop of vitamin E and add one-half teaspoon of cod liver oil (or administer with a dropper if your cat prefers).

This way you can add all these supplements without having to take five different jars out of the refrigerator twice a day. I give the measurements by the can of food because it's easier to mix when the can is freshly opened and the contents are soft. You'll probably have leftover food (if you are feeding less than five cats). Store the leftover food in a glass container with a cover and refrigerate. *Do not store in the can.* Molecular changes occur between the food and the can once it is opened. I use a glass container to store the leftover food because so much suspicion has been thrown on plastic dishes and containers that finicky owners avoid them, just to be on the safe side. A peanut butter jar is good; a pickled-artichoke jar is perfect. Some imported jams come in jars that are especially pleasing to the eye and hand. Here's a perfect excuse to splurge on one of them and then keep the jar as your permanent cat food storage jar for the refrigerator.

You can buy all the ingredients for the Vita-Mineral Mix at a health food store. After implementing this regime for one month, approximately 85 percent of my clients noticed the following changes: dandruff gone, oiliness diminishing and disappearing, matting diminishing and disappearing, shine appearing, texture becoming thick, rich and plushy. Of the other 15 percent, most noticed the changes after two, three, or six months because the cats were older, had a slower metabolism, or because the owners were slower to make a complete change in diet. For example, some owners, instead of removing the food after a half hour, would leave the food for as much as an hour and a half for the first couple of weeks. Other owners, whose cats were "hooked" on one of the really low-quality foods, spent the first couple of weeks mixing the old food with the new food, gradually diminishing the former lower-quality food until the cat was eating only the high-quality food.

Many of my clients, on seeing the spectacular results in their cat's furs, decided to include the same supplements in their own diets—as I myself do. If you're one of those people who wash your hair not because it's dirty but because it's lank or oily, I suggest you give it a try. You will also appreciate the effect on your fingernails and the whites of your eyes.

Many of my clients who also own dogs have applied the same diet to their cat's canine friends, and all have experienced the same happy results. I am not surprised. I am not an expert on canine nutrition but a high-quality diet will benefit any animal. The dog's basic requirements differ only slightly from the cat's. Dogs are a bit more like us humans in that they can be vegetarians if all the essential amino acids are supplied; also, they need a bit less fat than cats. Foods of Nature canned foods are suitable for both dogs and cats.

With any animal, it's very important to remove food after a half hour, leaving only water available between meals. This way the internal organs will all be well supplied with blood. Removing food between meals keeps your pet youthful and spry. My Priscilla, at fifteen, was still the champion soccer player with a ping-pong ball. Her haunches were so shapely they drove Big Purr crazy. He'd try to nibble them at every opportunity. Priscilla, being a lady, would respond by hitting him in the head. And Priscilla only weighs four and a half pounds, to Purr's twelve.

How Much to Feed?

When asked about what amount to feed, I tell the owner I have to know the cat. Most people overfeed their cats. A cat's stomach, before it expands, is the size of a quarter or a fifty-cent piece. A cat who eats two tablespoonfuls of food at each meal is doing fine. An easy way to regulate the amount is to think of time rather than quantity. In other words, if your cat is healthy and of normal size, neither too fat nor too thin, then the sky's the limit for half an hour. Also, your cat will not be eating exactly the same amount every day of the year. Appetites vary with temperature, barometric pressure, and so on. It's easy for me to see the patterns because I see so many cats every day.

Owners who previously fed low-quality foods are often alarmed because their cats eat less of the new food. I explain to them that the cats have been overeating because their systems have been reaching for missing nutrients. The poor cats eat and eat the same low quality food, from which they can never get the nutrients they crave. Often, feeding low-quality food makes for obese cats. Because the new high-quality food is complete nutrition, the cats are satisfied. They are getting *quality* as opposed to *quantity*. Flabby cats tend to firm up—they don't necessarily lose a lot of weight—they just get a little smaller and more active.

Changing Over to the New Diet

One sacrifice that is the earmark of the true finicky owner is that that owner takes the responsibility and acknowledges the fact that he or she is indeed smarter than the cat. I have discussed the various reasons cats can be hooked on an undesirable diet. Just the fact that "Familiarity breeds contentment in a cat" is enough to hook them on almost anything—simply because it is familiar.

When I see new clients and give instructions for an optimum diet, I always take care that they understand that I fully expect them to be calling me. It is normal during the first month or two for some question to arise. I am especially careful to make this crystal clear to owners who have previously left food available between meals. Although not a psychologist, I have observed that leaving food available is with some people a deep psychological need. Removing the food is indeed a very real sacrifice on the owners' part that they make out of a deep love. I know in advance that these people may cheat a little, and if they do and if the cat is hooked on something, I expect them to call and say, "She's not eating the new food—she has eaten nothing in five days." I will tell you now what I always tell them—if you leave any food around between meals I cannot help you because the cat will not be hungry at mealtime. "But I'm away all day," they say. Never mind—go back and read the very beginning of this chapter and, if you still want to leave food around while you're gone, you're defeated before you start. You might as well skip the rest of the chapter. Such behavior on the part of the owner is selfish and childish. I have my own term to describe the position of a cat belonging to such a person—I call them "working cats."

To the owners who confess their weakness and vow to turn over a new leaf, I give the following advice: All six veterinarians with whom I've worked agree on this—no one has ever heard of a cat who starved to death while something edible was available twice a day. Some cats will hold out from three to five days before taking a nibble. They may cry and complain. A few creative types that I've known walk over to the dish; very obviously sniff it, then turn around and proceed to scratch the floor as if they were trying to cover excrement. Such behavior may be hard to resist if you do not have the thought firmly in your conscious mind that you love your animals dearly and want them to stay with you alive and well for as many years as possible.

The cat sitters I supply to owners who travel are frequently faced with the assignment of making the dietary changeover while the owner is gone. They have a thorough grounding in the nutritional aspects of cat care, along with everything else. And, because their love of cats is a love of all cats, no matter who owns them, they're in a good position to remain emotionally detached so that they can do what is best for the cat without involving any psychological needs of their own. Here's what they do.

First, present the new food—the ideal diet. Keep the thought in your conscious mind of the nutritional soundness of the diet and how delicious it is. (Most cats adore yeast and kelp, not to mention cod liver oil.) Your own vibes of approval will be communicated to your cats. If you're really handling your conscious thoughts properly, you yourself will be salivating when you put that plate on the floor. Do what is natural, then—smack your lips, swallow, say you wish you had a delicious dinner like that, then leave them alone. Start your own dinner, wash the dishes, or go read a book. If the cats refuse the food, first of all ascertain whether or not the cats have eaten anything. Half a teaspoonful per cat is an acceptable amount. (Don't put so much food on the plate that you won't be able to tell how much they have eaten. Give them only a tablespoonful or two.) They'll eat more next time—because they won't be eating between meals. But let's say the cats eat nothing. Not one morsel passes their lips. After forty-five minutes, cheerfully clean away the food and casually forget the whole incident completely. If they ask for food between meals, give them extra love, cuddling, and play instead. Active play is especially good because it will work up an appetite. Repeat this procedure for a minimum of four meals; after all, that's only two days. A fast of two days is extremely beneficial because many old wastes and toxins will be excreted by the body quickly. That's what a fast is—it's *fast*.

An owner of a positively obese cat often asks me in a tremulous voice, full of sincere concern, "But what if she skips a meal—what if she doesn't eat anything at all—what shall I do?" I look from the huge animal sprawled at our feet and back at the owner, and I reply, very solemnly, "Applaud." This tack always works. The owner laughs.

After you've done your duty for four meals, you deserve a pat on the back. Ninety-eight percent of the cats will have made the changeover by this time. (Eighty percent of the cats welcome the new food the moment it is set on the floor—they dive into it. This section is only for the benefit of those poor creatures who have no appetite because their food was left available between meals or they were hooked on some undesirable product.)

If your cats are in that small percentage that has not eaten the new food after two days they will now be hungry—and they will jump at any compromise you offer. So, fine—we'll compromise. I'm not made of stone. But first let's try the old "special treats ploy." The technique here is to offer them something that is utterly delicious—it can be something that you would not feed every day, something that is not in itself complete nutrition. For example, you might try baby food meat or broiled chicken thigh. Be sure to add at least half a teaspoonful of Vita-Mineral Mix, or, at the very least, half a teaspoonful of bran, so it won't constipate them. You are breaking the problem into two parts: first, getting them to eat something besides the old food and then, second, getting them to start eating the ideal diet. By feeding these special treat foods, you are breaking the old habit. The next step is to start mixing the special treat food with the ideal diet, gradually increasing the percentage of the new food.

- *First day.* Only the special treat food.
- *Second, third, and fourth days.* Three parts special treat food to one part ideal diet.
- *Next five days.* Fifty-fifty ratio.
- *Next five days.* One part special treat food to three parts ideal diet.

Then you're home free. Caution—do not use the food your cat is hooked on. I have seen this method of mixing the old diet with the new ultimately work after fasting a cat two days but the number of days allowed before making each ratio change must be doubled and even then there are usually setbacks. Try your best not to use any really undesirable food as a bribe. If you're going to stoop to fish, at least make sure it's not tuna. And, to avoid getting your cats hooked on anything ever again, make sure you feed a variety of flavors.

Nature moves slowly. You will not perceive at first the change that is occurring within the cat—the condition of the walls of the veins, the new chemical balance of the blood, which feeds every organ including the brain and the nerves. The resultant youthfulness, the mellowing of the disposition—will creep in like the unfolding of a rose, which can be seen clearly in speeded-up photography but cannot be perceived when you yourself simply stand and look at it. Yet intellectually you know the rose is blooming because you've already seen the results many times before. You could assure anyone who has not seen a full-blown rose that yes, truly, that bud will become, in time, a ravishing bloom. It will be like that with the diet once you see it in your cats. You'll be able to pass it on to others and benefit other cats. In fact, the more trouble you have, the more pitfalls you overcome, the better equipped you will be to help others over the rough and thorny parts.

Other Beneficial Side Effects of High-Quality Diet

One thing I did not expect was the way the diet influenced temperament. The minerals and B vitamins apparently had a favorable effect on the nerves. "She came right out into the living room when company was there" is the sort of comment I hear after a couple of months on the new diet. "He's starting to play again," "She doesn't hiss at the maid"—in other words, the temperament seems to go toward the golden mean. Nervous cats calm down; lazy cats perk up. Well, why not? Metabolism is speeded up; old waste products are being eliminated; the body is cleaner inside; irritating toxins are disappearing day by day; and health-building nutrients are in plentiful supply. The body of such a cat has a high resistance to both disease and stress.

Another lovely side effect is the perfume exuded by the furs of a healthy cat. To the joys of softness, luster, warmth, and shininess, add also the dimension of delightful perfume.

Vitamins

I do not give multiple vitamins every day as a habit. Under normal circumstances, I give them twice a week at irregular intervals. I don't want the cats to become dependent on the vitamin pill and lower their ability to assimilate the nutrients from the whole food. Also, I feel more secure giving vitamin sources where the vitamins are not isolated—for example, instead of giving a vitamin B pill, I would rather give yeast and toasted wheat germ, which are extremely rich in all the B vitamins but which also contain all the other little elements that nature intended her children to ingest along with those B vitamins. But if your cats get ringworm, fleas, upper respiratory infection, or any infestation or disease, give them a vitamin pill four or five times a week until the battle is over. Double the Vita-Mineral Mix in their food. If you ever sneak between-meal snacks to your cats for heaven's sake stop during illness—no matter how nutritious and fabulous they seem to you. To fight an infection or infestation, the body needs that time between meals to cleanse itself of the poisons as much as it needs that super-nutritious food you are giving at mealtime. Crush and add a quarter clove of garlic to the food once a day or give as you would a vitamin pill, after the meal. Vitamins are always given after the meal, when the stomach is full. Get your multiple vitamins from the veterinarian and make sure they are tablets or liquid. There is a variety of vitamin that comes in a tube and is suspended in a mineral oil. It resembles brown Vaseline. This is not good because mineral oil washes vitamins A, D, and E right out of the system. (There is also a feline laxative that does the same thing. Mineral oil should be be used very, very rarely and only under specific instructions from the vet.) My cats adore Pet Tabs and FeloBits. They're about as big as a nickel and, although they smell perfectly horrible to me, I have to be careful how I present them, because if I place the tablets too close together on the floor my sweet and gregarious cats are not above hissing and swatting each other to try to get the lion's share. They find them truly delicious. It's also acceptable to mix vitamins into the food if your cat indicates this preference.

Additional Food Supplements

Owners frequently ask about variety in the cat's diet. Cats in the wild eat sprouting grass and grains; they steal eggs from a nest; they eat a variety of different birds, frogs, lizards, rodents, and who knows what sorts of vegetables and fruits. There are many similar food supplements you can add to your cat's meal or give as a side dish:

- A teaspoonful of freshly chopped alfalfa sprouts (high in nutrients and still full of life when cats eat them)
- Steamed broccoli tops
- Peas, corn, squash, or other steamed vegetables
- A soft-boiled egg
- Cooked meat or poultry (remember, no ham or pork and no poultry bones)
- An olive
- A cantaloupe ball
- A sliver of pizza

- A whole wheat bread crust, buttered or not
- A string of spaghetti (only one, unless it is whole grain)

Ask your cats, even about the most unlikely foods. If they crave something containing sugar, white flour, and so on, give them no more than half a teaspoonful, and only once a week. Such forbidden treats can be useful for hiding medication if, heaven forbid, your cat should become ill and have to take a pill. (See Chapter 7 for more on pilling.)

I mix high-quality foods such as alfalfa in with the meal at least once a week. Every day is even better. I'm told that alfalfa sprouts tend to satisfy the most incorrigible houseplant nibbler, too.

The Superfinicky Owner's "I'll-Do-Anything-for-My-Cat" Diet

The superfinicky owner who prepares his or her own cat food from scratch really has a firm grip with both hands on that health-bestowing magic wand. It's simple to do; the time you spend making up food will be saved later because it's faster to open a zip-lock baggie than to open a can. Also, your cats will be healthier on their tailor-made diet and will require less nursing care, pilling, and ferrying to the veterinarian in later years. And—surprise!—the cost is the same or even less than commercial canned cat food. I suggest you first try it for a month, because that gives you time to get it down to a quick, easy routine and it gives your cats time to show evidence of the upgraded diet with upgraded coat, eyes, and temperament.

Because you are making up your own formula, you can tailor the texture as well as the taste and nutritional content of your cats' meals. Most cats like a smooth, creamy consistency such as baby food, so at first blend or mash everything well. Then you can hold out a few chunks of cooked meat and baked carrot to mix in at the end. Many cats find chomping on lumps exciting. You'll have to ask your own cats' opinion on that.

If you can manage to get all organically grown, unsprayed products, that, of course, is best. Commercial pesticides used on vegetables are poisonous, and chemical fertilizers lower vitamin content considerably. The hormones and antibiotics injected as a matter of course into all the meat and poultry available on the open market are better left right where they are—on the open market, not in your cat's stomach.

Remember, you won't be paying more for the food because you will be serving quality proteins instead of quantity. One organic chicken will last two cats for two weeks when used in the proper ratio with grain, bean, egg and vegetables. The proteins you will use are so nicely balanced that not as much animal protein is needed. This careful protein balance yields the added dividend of saving the cats' kidneys and keeping them functioning efficiently into old age.

If you have no blender, just chop and mash—or, as a second choice, you can use the organic baby foods (meat, vegetable, and cereals) available at health food stores. If you don't have such a store in your area, you'll have to fall back on what the standard grocery store can supply. It's a bit overcooked, but you will still be serving meals far, far above the canned cat foods in nutritional quality and freshness.

Here's the basic recipe for the "I'll-Do-Anything-for-My-Cat" Diet:

2 to 4 parts animal protein (2 parts is better for older cats—some cats insist on 4 parts animal protein as a matter of taste)

1 part bean, tofu, or milk products (milk products only if they don't give your cat diarrhea)

3 parts whole grain

2 parts vegetables, lightly cooked or raw

Broth, or water, or vegetable juice to taste

The following list gives a few suggestions in each of the four categories. You can use one or several foods together in each of the categories as long as you keep to the basic ratio just presented.

Animal Protein

Chicken, cooked (no bones except neck vertebrae)

Beef, cooked

Lamb, cooked

Egg, soft-boiled or cooked other ways (a little ground shell is very good)

Organic baby food (no pork)

Note: Egg is a wonderful protein source but should not comprise the entire protein measure because it is low in the amino acid taurine, which is essential to cats. Chicken is at the top of the meat list because it is high in taurine and is very easily digested by cats. It is also a natural cat food, because wild cats kill and eat birds and other fowl.

Bean, Tofu, or Milk Products

Beans, lentils, or chick peas (garbanzo beans or ceci beans), soaked overnight and then simmered three hours, *unsalted*

Tofu (bean curd), cooked or raw

Tempeh, sauteed in chunks or mashed

Soy grits, soaked and boiled

Cottage cheese, yogurt, milk, or cheese (find out if your cat is able to digest milk products by serving each one separately before you try using any of them in the food mixture)

Whole Grains

Oatmeal, raw, soaked overnight (or soak 2 to 3 days for more enzymes) or cooked

Barley, cooked

Millet, cooked

Brown rice, cooked

Kasha, cooked

Sweet corn, cooked

Whole grain bread or granola (no honey or sugar)

Vegetables (fresh are preferred; frozen is second best)

Baked or steamed:
  Orange squash
  Carrot
  Broccoli
  Peas
  Green beans
  Zucchini
  Yam or potato

Raw chopped:
  Sprouts: alfalfa, mung bean, or soy (All sprouts are valuable, but must be added at the last minute before serving. Don't store the food with the sprouts already added.)
  Grated carrot
  Chopped parsley
  Chopped greens

When you first begin making your own cat food, use a small measure—a tablespoon or even a teaspoon to equal one part. Make up relatively small amounts of the food until you hit on three or four combinations that your cat really enjoys. Then begin making large amounts, using a quarter cup or even a cup as your one-part measure. Store enough food for one meal in a zip-lock baggie. If you have one cat, put one serving in a baggie; if you have three cats, three servings. Store them in the freezer and thaw as needed by dropping the baggie into a bowl of hot tap water.

For each cat, add a teaspoonful of Vita-Mineral Mix. Do this just before serving because the mix, like sprouts, loses much virtue if frozen or heated. Also remember to give each cat a dropperful of cod liver oil three times a week and a drop from a 100-unit vitamin E capsule.

Feeding Kittens

If you are so rash as to adopt a young kitten, you must realize that kittens eat much more frequently than do grown cats. Their little stomachs are minute, and their metabolism is very rapid. The smaller the animal, the more rapid the metabolism. Birds, for example, spend practically every waking hour finding food to fuel their bodies. A kitten between six and ten weeks old requires five or six meals a day. From ten weeks to four months, four meals are required; three meals until six months; and then two meals a day after the age of six months.

Kittens should not be taken from the mother before they are six weeks old. Eight weeks is much kinder. Otherwise, they get oral fixations and spend their lives sucking buttons and ear lobes. Although this may seem cute to some people, it saddens anyone who knows that it is a symptom of maladjustment due to too-early weaning.

A kitten, once weaned, can eat the same food you feed any healthy cat, as discussed earlier in this chapter. A growing kitten needs a high-protein diet, and that's what this is. You might like to add an extra quarter-teaspoonful of butter once a day because kittens can use more fat. Also add some water to make the consistency easier for the kitten to handle.

If, through no fault of yours or the kittens, you should suddenly find yourself with a kitten of less than six weeks on your hands, then you've got special problems. The employees of a printing office once called me to say that they had discovered a sodden shoebox in the gutter out front with four newborn kittens in it. They had already called the SPCA and a couple of other humane shelters. Each time, they received the same advice: "Kill the kittens quickly and painlessly—kittens that young cannot survive." At that time I knew next to nothing about feline nutrition. "Fools rush in"—I hopped a subway down there and accepted the four kittens. Three of them were making sounds. The fourth was dead when I got there. They really were newborn—I doubt if they had ever even nursed.

I called a vet, who gave me the same advice that the animal shelters had given the office people. When I insisted that I wanted to try to save them, he referred me to a very large pet store that sold powdered queen's milk (a queen is a female cat). My friend Mark came over and assisted in keeping the kittens warm. We held them under our sweaters next to our skin. We couldn't find a doll baby bottle so we used a rubber ear syringe made for a baby's ears. We lost two more kittens in twenty-four hours despite feeding every two hours, stroking, warmth, and all our good wishes.

At that time I had two female cats, both neutered. And, although I wasn't sure whether they would accept a kitten or kill it, I was desperate and decided to take a chance. I put the remaining little black male on the carpet in front of Lee-la and Pixie, my two Siamese. That's what I should have done in the first place. Lee-la curled her body around him, and she and Pixie both went to work with those rough Siamese tongues. Lee-la licked and massaged the kitten's lower abdomen with grim determination until, in less than one minute, that little mite had passed a stool. If it's going in one end and it's coming out the other, that's a favorable sign. Pixie cleaned his eyes and his ears to her satisfaction, despite the little one's feeble protests. And, as she began licking his back, the little black male fell asleep. At that point I felt safe in giving him a name, because it looked like the odds in his favor had just risen a good bit. Being newly into yoga, I decided to call him Jai, which means "victory" in Sanskrit. Sanskrit words impart their vibrations to anyone who hears them, and I figured that "Jai" was just what this little squirt needed.

Jai continued to get queen's milk for three weeks. He also continued to get bathed and cuddled and generally mothered by my two prim Siamese ladies. At three weeks of age, I began mixing baby food (lamb and carrots) with the milk. I got him to lick out of a plate by putting some of this food on my finger and dirtying his nose with it. I put just a drop on the tip of his nose, and his little tongue would automatically come out to lick it off. It tasted good. He looked for more and found it on my finger. I kept dipping my finger into the dish and offering it to him. Each time I made him reach closer and closer to the dish by moving my finger down towards it. Being bright, he soon figured out that my finger was a middle-man he could do away with by going straight to the source. On the vet's advice, I stopped the queen's milk at four weeks and changed to Similac human infant formula. I mixed this with baby food oatmeal, carrots, and beef or lamb. At five weeks, I had intended to gradually introduce grown-up cat food. However, Jai found it for himself and attacked his foster mothers' plates with such gusto that my problem became one of preventing his overeating.

Until Jai was six weeks old, I must have fed him six to eight meals a day. Jai remained petite up through six months. He had a mature conformation, but his size was that of an eight-week-old kitten. He looked like a miniature cat. Soon afterward he was adopted by a nice young couple who moved to California. There he had a yard, sunshine, and air—and, before long, a girlfriend (both cats were neutered). I was informed through mutual friends that my tiny Jai was tiny no more. He grew and filled out to become a big, strapping male, the terror of chipmunks.

The Litter Box

There is no area of cat care that is as potentially distressing to both cats and their owners as the litter box. Neither party wants a smelly, dirty litter pan. But, unfortunately, even the most caring owners have found themselves trapped in the old, established litter box system. Well, take heart—there is an alternative.

The Litter Box Problem

I have seen litter box setups that must have cost a small fortune. Pet shops have a formidable array—some with plastic domes, plastic liners, even built-in sieves and strainers. For litter, people turn to clay, cedar chips, sawdust, and newspaper. Litter boxes are moved about from the kitchen to the bathroom to behind the bed to under the coffee table. Their number can range from one to ten. Because of the random wetting problem, Persian cats are thrown out, given back, given away, and killed. The litter box is clearly a headache for both the cats and their owners—unless you know how to simplify the system.

In order to devise an acceptable system for both cat and owner, I went back to what Dr. Rowan had once told me, "Stick as close as you can to nature, and you won't go too far wrong." He was discussing food and feeding at the time, but I felt that the same concept might be applied to the litter box. So how does a wild cat behave in this respect?

The cat's urine is very concentrated, and the smell is strong. Because this smell could attract predators to the nest, cats in the wild always urinate far away from their habitat or any place of activity. They do not urinate where they sleep, eat, hunt, or play. Young kittens are frequently and thoroughly cleaned by the mother, who then swallows any waste matter, passing it through her own system to be neatly disposed of later with her own body wastes. With this kind of training in cleanliness from birth, is it any wonder that cats are fastidious about where they urinate?

Many a random wetting problem begins when the litter box is placed near the food dish or a favorite resting place. That litter box looks great, but the cats would have to be insane to soil near the area where they eat or rest. So the cat simply begins to search for an acceptable place to use. (See more on random wetting in Chapter 7.)

Cats hide their urine. They are not comfortable or at peace when they have to stand on old, half-wet litter to void again. Cats, in fact, have a universally accepted reputation for neatness. That's one of the reasons why we find them so attractive.

You might even say they are very much like us. Let us imagine that any one of us should walk into a bathroom and find that the toilet had already been used—but not flushed. What does one automatically do? And even if you do not flush before using it, do you then have to stand inside the dirty toilet to use it? And, even if you did, *you* do not have long, silky bloomers to dangle down into the smelly mess—ugh!

Cats cannot flush their own toilet; you have to do it for them. Put the litter pan in the bathroom, and when you flush for yourself flush for them too. Persian cats have especially long, fluffy bloomers, and they are notoriously fastidious about what might get caught in their furs.

Surprisingly, I have found that the people with the smelliest apartments and homes were not those with the random wetting problem but those with the largest, deepest litter boxes. It soon became apparent that, the deeper the bed of litter, the worse the smell and the higher the incidence of random wetting.

The Requirements for a Litter Box

Now let us list the requirements for the litter box, from both the cats' viewpoint and ours.

Cat	Owner
Clean	Clean
Odorless	Odorless

Convenient	Convenient
Out of the way	Out of the way
	Inexpensive
	Sanitary

You'll notice that our requirements are the same as the cats with the addition of inexpensive (because we must maintain the facility) and sanitary (because that is our responsibility—pussycats don't know about germs).

I began my research by simply trying first to satisfy the cats' requirements. The method I ended up with turned out automatically to fulfill all of the owner's requirements as well. Here is one case where the very best is also the easiest, most sanitary, and by far the cheapest.

An Easy, Convenient, and Effective System

Put the litter box near the toilet. This is out of the way and convenient. The cat doesn't eat or sleep near the toilet and you can clean it every time you go into the bathroom. The tub is a good place for the box, because it is then easy to brush up any litter that is kicked out.

A small plastic dishpan is the easiest litter box. It's just the right size and has fairly high sides. Don't buy one of those expensive covered litter boxes—it's not convenient for you or your cat. The dome prevents you from seeing whether it needs cleaning or not. Also, because cats squat upright, a low roof impairs free movement of the bowels and bladder. In addition, the small pan is much easier to handle when you're cleaning it.

Any commercial litter is fine. You and your cat can work that out between you. I find clay (Hartz Mountain is my first choice) to be the most efficient. However, I have met one or two rare Persians who prefer newspaper because it doesn't cling to their bloomers. In that case you wouldn't flush; you'd have to incinerate it.

Just keep a giant tablespoon or serving spoon, one with *no holes* or slits in it, on a hook or in a glass or mug near the box. Whenever you pass the bathroom, take a quick look at the box. If you see a covered mound or a little wet circle, which is like the tip of an iceberg, pick the litter box up and gently shake all the dry litter to one end exposing the wet clump. Then, take your giant tablespoon and remove every bit of the wet clump and flush it away. The remaining litter is left clean and uncontaminated, so shake it evenly across the pan again and replace the spoon in its holder after rinsing it in clean flush water.

Use only one-quarter to three-quarters of an inch of litter at a time, *no deeper.* You want the wet to hit the bottom and clump, not spread and seep through the other litter to contaminate it and make it smell. If you're going to be gone eight hours or more and you have more than a couple of cats, do as I do. I have one pan for each two cats and clean them on arising, before leaving, when I return, and before bed. It takes about fifteen seconds per pan per cleaning.

Don't buy one of those commercial "litter scoops" full of holes and slits. They must have been invented by someone who wanted you to use lots and lots of litter. Supposedly they are to be used to lift out the "solid matter." Well, if you just stop to think about it, the solid matter is not the problem. The stool will smell bad for about three minutes, but then it's dry. The cats can easily step around that. It's the wetness that really smells; it's the wet parts that breed germs; and it's the wet parts that make it impossible for a cat to use the box without stepping on old urine.

If you try to remove the wet litter with a commercial litter scoop, you'll have some mess on your hands with half the wet bits of litter filtering down onto the floor, the toilet seat and, worst of all, back into the clean litter to contaminate it and make it smell.

Don't make the mistake of putting too much litter in the box. I have come across great, huge litter pans with ten to fifteen pounds of litter in them. These pans are always the smelliest, because the urine doesn't hit the bottom and clump but continues to permeate the whole ten pounds like a miasmic fog. The rule is "If the litter smells, *use less* and *clean more often.*"

And don't line your nice, smooth plastic pan with anything. Newspaper does not deodorize; it smells. Those messy plastic liners always form little wrinkles where wet litter hides to smell and breed germs. Fifty percent of the time the cat's claw puts a hole in it anyway, and the urine drains through and sits there in a puddle under the liner where there is no litter to absorb the odor.

With my method, you need to change and wash the whole pan only once or twice a week. When they do the complete cleaning, finicky owners will feel as if they are cleaning an already clean litter box. Because they have scooped out the wet clumps so often, there is absolutely no odor about the plastic box. At the most, there might be a little dot of dry stool clinging to the side of the pan. With my litter boxes, after dumping out what little litter remains, I swish it out with water, dump that out, sprinkle in a little powdered cleanser, and scrub it inside and out with the toilet brush.

Finally, I rinse like crazy. If you think I'm finicky about food, I become absolutely rabid about any kind of chemical a cat might get on his paws or fur and lick off. No residue of soap or cleaner must be left in the box.

There is just no need for those deodorant sprays made especially for "kitty's box." Three of my pussycat clients in one household came down with a stubborn case of foot fungus, the cause of which was finally traced to an aerosol spray for the box. I explained to that owner that if you smell an odor from the box you're doing something wrong—usually using too much litter and not cleaning frequently enough. Using deodorant spray on a dirty box is like spraying perfume on a dirty body—one doesn't.

I might add that there are some owners who, instead of scooping out the wet with a spoon, prefer to dump the whole thing three or four times a day. They put even less litter in the box—say an eighth of an inch—and swish the box out with water each time. I call these people "super-finicky," and their cats are absolutely ecstatic about this system. With this new litter box system, get ready to buy a lot less litter. You will be amazed at how little you will be using.

Even if you have more than one cat, you should be able to identify each cat's stool in order to be sure that each cat puts out a stool once or twice a day. There are many instances when knowing what's going in one end and what's coming out the other is worth its weight in gold. It gives the finicky owner peace of mind. Finicky owners as a group have the highest standards of cat health, fitness, and happiness.

If you notice a change in the consistency of one of the cat's stools, immediately try to figure out what caused the change. Did the cat eat a milk product that made the stool runny? Did the cat eat more than his or her share of chicken neck vertebrae, which turned the stool into a series of hard little balls? If you don't know the cause for a change in stool consistency, then watch the cat carefully for the appearance of any other adverse symptoms such as copious water drinking, loss of appetite, lethargy, and so on. Hopefully the stool will return to normal tomorrow, and you can breathe easily again.

Training Kittens to Use the Litter Box

The mother cat always toilet trains the kittens herself, so you never have to worry—well, hardly ever. On one or two rare occasions, I have received calls for help from people with a litter of kittens who were wetting and dirtying outside the box. Because "everyone knows" that you don't have to housebreak a cat, the amazed owners wondered if these accidents were happening just because the kittens were still too young. The answer is no. Under normal circumstances, at no time will a kitten or cat dirty or wet outside the box. Abnormal circumstances include the loss of the mother before she completes their training, inaccessibility of a litter box, or unsanitary conditions in the litter box.

Years ago I ran up against yet another reason for this problem. Triple Champion Purr-du's Lee-la of Mar Wal was a lovely chocolate-point Siamese. To see her was to lose your heart. She was all purrs and cuddling and posing and sweetness—the darling of all who beheld her. Lee-la knew she was a winner, and because the world had always treated her royally she had come to expect the very best at all times. She had never been frightened, so she did not know fear. Lee-la was not the brightest cat I ever met but with all that charm and beauty, who cared?—until her kittens began to use the rugs for a toilet. The family was shocked; Lee-la was unconcerned. Because Lee-la didn't know what fear was, she lacked that basic instinct to protect the young by teaching them to bury their wastes where the smell would never draw dangerous predators to the area. Her six kittens were happy, healthy, and absolutely beautiful, but Lee-la's laissez-faire policy was driving the family to distraction.

The solution to this, as in so many situations, is found on a very primitive level. First let's examine exactly how, in nature, this automatic kitten training actually does occur; then, if necessity arises, a human can duplicate it.

Newborn kittens pass wastes while lying on their backs after nursing when they feel the mother's tongue stroking down their belly and out along the tail. The tiny amount of waste is simply cleaned away by the sweep of the mother's tongue and swallowed by the mother. The procedure is a study in efficiency, cleanliness, and safety. The mother disposes of the wastes a safe distance away from the nest, passing them out of her body with her own excrement.

When the kittens are old enough to walk a little distance and squat without falling over, the mother will lead them to a preferred place (the litter box, in the home situation), and as they stand in the litter she begins to lick the genital area, thus triggering the response of urinating and passing stool.

When the tiny stools and thimblefuls of urine are all lying in the litter box, the mother then rallies her kittens to a jolly group effort of covering up the wastes. The kittens dutifully scratch and sniff and circle around with such vigor that the litter usually flies in all directions, showering the rug and floor for several feet around. Then the proud parent chases them all out of the box and the group runs pell-mell away, putting a safe distance between themselves and the area where lingering smell could attract a predator.

So, if some crucial part of the training is missing, the solution becomes obvious. Someone must supply the missing element—in the case of Lee-la, the mother's tongue that triggers the response to deposit wastes in the litter.

Here's how it's done. After each meal, which is the usual time for the kittens to pass wastes, carry the kitten or kittens into the litter box. Dip your finger into a cup of hot water so it will feel as much as possible like a warm, moist tongue. Then place the finger between the kitten's hindlegs so that the tip of your finger rests against the stomach. Stroke the finger backward against the kitten's tummy and up across the genitals and anus once or twice. Dip your finger in the hot water again and repeat, or go on to the next kitten. When a kitten begins to squat and pass wastes, gently pet its forehead as a sign of encouragement and approval. At the end of the exercise, cover the wastes with your fingertip, lift the kittens out of the box and lure them away with a string or a toy.

Lee-la used to love to watch the performance from her queenly perch up on the sink. She would purr loudly the whole time. Indeed, I had the feeling that by the time those kittens were finally litter trained, Triple Champion Purr-du's Lee-la of Mar Wal was just as proud of me as she was of her kittens.

The Scratching Post

It is a sad fact that many unaware owners have had their cats declawed simply because they thought it was the only way to protect their furniture and carpeting. Fortunately, this is not the case. I hope the declawing operation will become obsolete as owners learn to meet their cats' needs by supplying a scratching post that the cats find irresistible.

Cats Need to Scratch

Cats should be encouraged to scratch because all the musculature, from the claws through the legs and shoulders and down the back, are exercised and toned when the cat scratches to clean and sharpen his claws. A cat who doesn't scratch has underdeveloped muscles. All wild cats love a good claw at a nice, rough tree. This means the scratching post should be rough, too.

Unfortunately, most posts in pet shops are made to attract owners instead of cats, because it's the owners who walk in with money to buy the post. Ninety-nine percent of all owners are attracted by a soft-looking, fluffy-wuffy scratching post. The *cat* should be fluffy-wuffy—the *post* should be rough and coarse. We may not find it practical to bring a tree trunk into the home or a small apartment, but there are other alternatives. Cats are attracted to something rough, like the back of a good rug or, heaven forbid, Great-Grandmother's needlepoint footstool. What the cat needs is a post so wonderfully rough and scratchy that Great-Grandmother's needlepoint footstool becomes second rate by comparison.

Happily, such a post is available by mail from the Felix Katnip Tree Company, 416 Smith Street, Seattle, Washington 98109 (as of this writing, it is $20.25, postage included). When you order, ask for the extra-large model *sisal* scratching post. Sisal is a harsh, scratchy hemp product. It stands about three feet high and is fixed in a square base.

I have seen my big Purr take a flying leap off the table to land on the top of the post. Balancing nicely, he extends the claws of all four feet and blissfully digs in. A far-off look of ecstasy suffuses his countenance as he sways. It is the most subtle of dances. As the clawing goes deeper and the dance steps become more pronounced, Purr's post trembles with the violence of his digging and pulling. But it never tips over, because the Felix post has a good firm base.

Many cats are declawed *because of* fluffy scratching posts. Because fluffy scratching posts do not fulfill their purpose from the cats' point of view, they go to your furniture in desperation. Then the owners complain, "I tried a post, and he refuses to use it." It's not the cat's fault—it's the fault of the post. Either it is too fluffy and soft or too rickety or small. The trick is to give your cats a post they can't resist.

If you want to make your own scratching post, use a rug with a rough backing and put the backing side out. Also, make sure the whole thing is secure and won't wobble or fall over. If you meet these two criteria, you're home free. Even the backside of a piece of carpet laid on the floor is better than a fluffy-wuffy post. If you've already been taken in by the fluffy-wuffy variety, why not recover it with carpet turned backside out? This will work fine as long as you have a large, firm base.

When Your Scratching Post Arrives

In case you decide to purchase a Felix Katnip Tree, I am including instructions here on how to set it up because the Felix Company includes none, assuming apparently that the method of assembly is blatantly obvious. After all, there are only three pieces to deal with: the post, the base, and a little metal wedge. However, during the excitement precipitated by the arrival of the post, even the most level-headed and responsible of people can forget themselves and inadvertently toss away the all-important little metal wedge, without which the post has no stability. I have seen so many wobbly, insecure, improperly assembled Felix posts that I must caution you—*don't throw away that little metal wedge!*

There is no need to plan an introduction of the cats to their new post. Here's what usually happens when the Felix Katnip Tree arrives: If you just leave the package lying on the floor inside the door, your cats will soon trot over to have a good sniff. The odor of catnip wafting from that parcel is absolutely fascinating and not to be resisted. If they start clawing at it wrapped as it is, you can help by snipping strings and peeling away the cardboard cover (there are two layers of wrapping).

Now, only the brown paper stands between the cats and their Katnip Tree. They may begin to attack it with violence, ripping and tearing at it with teeth and claws. By now, some of the very potent catnip will have fallen out. The catnip may propel your cats onto Cloud Nine, where they will enter a state of ecstasy, rolling about on their backs from side to side and rubbing their cheeks against the wonderful package. It is not unusual to see cats grab the post with front claws, hugging it to them, while raking it viciously with the hind claws. Their excitement can be felt like the temperature in the room. The catnip may not do much for you, but your cats' wild abandon will tell its own story.

In order to stretch out your cats' pleasure and anticipation of this new toy, leave the post wrapped as it is for an hour or even a day and just let them enjoy ripping at the paper and tape and getting half-scratches at whatever bit of the post they expose. As a matter of fact, anytime you want your cats to do something, your best bet is to engineer the circumstances so that you keep the cats in the position of asking for it or reaching for it rather than presenting it to them on a silver platter, or even worse, thrusting it on them.

Perhaps the next day, when your cats again begin to attack the parcel, you can go ahead and get down on the rug and help them as they rip and tear the wrapping paper away, exposing completely that irresistible scratchiness—the naked post dripping with powdered catnip. Once the post is completely exposed, the cats will probably pull the whole length of their bodies close against its primitive roughness and begin rubbing their cheeks against the sisal fabric and chewing on it. Go ahead—join the party. Scratch it yourself. What an intriguing sound for a pussycat's ears! Then scratch the cats. Really get into it, with your nails and your hands. You'll send them into fresh throes of sensual delight. Cloud Nine will be left far below. Their eyes may glaze over slightly, and they may utter low guttural sounds from deep in their throats. Do not be alarmed, it's normal when cats are totally focused on hitherto-undreamed-of pleasure.

In ten or fifteen minutes, the cats, thoroughly sated, will tumble into a heap somewhere to sleep it off. Now is a good time to assemble the post. Look for some tape around the wooden peg on the bottom of the post. Wrapped in that tape is the all-important little metal wedge. When the post is inserted in its base, this metal wedge is then pounded into the center of the peg, expanding it to fit snugly into the base. If you throw the tape away without removing the metal wedge, the post will go into the base all right, but when the cats stretch up, extending their eager claws to dig in, the whole contraption wiggles and wobbles and sometimes even falls apart on top of the cats. What a nasty shock! It's enough to put a cat off scratching posts for life. And all because one silly metal wedge was inadvertently thrown away.

Where to Put the Scratching Post

There are three possible ways to position the post:

1. In a corner, with the base touching two right-angle walls for security.
2. Next to Great-Grandmother's needlepoint footstool, so that when the cats go for the footstool they will see the post and, naturally, jump on the post.
3. On its side, like a tilt-board, because many highly bred or nervous cats can be extremely suspicious of anything new or strange.

If your cats do not immediately leap on the post and begin scratching like mad, you can (1) scratch the post yourself and tell them how much you enjoy the sensation or (2) lay the post on its side, pick the cats up, and stand them on the tilting post. Never grab cats by their legs or feet and force them onto the post. Cats hate that, and it will have a very negative effect—just the opposite of what you're trying to achieve. Just stroke firmly down their necks and backs so that you urge their bodies backward. Most cats dig their claws into the post as an expression of ecstasy. Alternate between scratching the post with your fingernails in front of them with the firm, stroking, pulling gesture down their backs. In other words, you are creating a situation where they feel ecstasy, and at the same time you are showing them how to express it.

Reinforcing Use of the Scratching Post

To reinforce the association of happiness with the post, work use of the post into other situations that are normally happy occasions, for example, your arrival home, before and after feeding, and/or before and after play time. When I'm caring for cats who are up for adoption, I make sure they are dedicated scratching post users so there is no danger of their ever being declawed by a misinformed future owner.

Every time I come home, the cats are happy and excited. But I don't pet them right away. First I run to the scratching post and begin scratching the top of the post with my nails and tell the cats how glad I am to be back and how much I missed them. In response, they all crowd in and begin clawing the post. As soon as they start clawing the post, I stop scratching it and start petting them, continuing my verbal assurances of love, interspersed with comments about how strong, lithe, and graceful they look while scratching the post. Because cats adore ritual and sameness, I further reinforce the pleasure of the situation by adding a key phrase. I always say, "Let's greet, let's greet" when I run from the door to the post.

Because "catch and kill" with the use of claws precedes eating in nature, you can also scratch the post before you prepare the cat's food, perhaps using a ritualistic phrase such as "Are you hungry?" "Is it time?" or something worked out by you and your cat. After eating, the phrase might be "Was it good?" The same principle can be used before and after play time.

Don't freshen the catnip on the post more than once a week, because otherwise the cats will become immune to its effects and will not react as strongly.

The Physical and Emotional Effects of Declawing

Many veterinarians do not explain the reality of the declawing operation to cat owners. Physically, realistically, it is precisely ten amputations. Moreover, it is ten complex amputations. The cat must remain under an anesthetic quite a long time. Anesthetizing a cat for even a short time is, as everyone knows, chancy. The claw is harder to remove than the tip joint of all ten of your fingers because you do not retract your fingertip. Your fingertip is not set into the joint below in a complex fashion. A cat's claw is. Someone once described declawing to me as "cutting pieces out of animal's bodies for convenience." I was absolutely horrified by the starkness of the way she faced this reality. People prefer not to discuss this so graphically in polite company. I apologize to those who already know the reality for reminding you of it and for bringing into your conscious mind again something so painful. But I have met too many loving owners who were never told, or who had the operation misrepresented to them only to find out, perhaps years after it was done, the truth about what they had actually done to the animal they adored. There are several veterinarians in New York City who refuse to do the operation and are happy to explain why.

The physical effect of declawing is gradual weakening of the muscles of the legs, shoulders, and back. Balance is impaired. The cat is 75 percent defenseless. Cats don't defend themselves with their teeth, they defend themselves with their claws.

The long-range effects are both physical and emotional. Because they are defenseless, declawed cats live in a constant state of stress. This is very draining. Because of the constant stress, the cats are more prone to get any disease. (See more on stress in Chapter 7.)

Declawed cats bite sooner and more often than cats that have their claws because they are more tense and nervous and because they no longer have their claws to use as a warning. The claws are their first line of defense. With that gone, they must resort to desperate measures—the use of their teeth. For that reason, a declawed cat is not one you would want to have around young children.

Newborn kittens until the age of three weeks or so have not yet learned to retract their claws. But once cats have reached that age, they begin to have control of their claws and can be trained to not use them on human flesh.

Declawed cats are much harder for a groomer or veterinarian to handle because of their highly nervous state and their proclivity for using teeth. Cats use claws as a mode of expression. We humans have sounds and words and laughter, but cats say, "Mmmm, this feels good" by gently kneading their claws. When I'm grooming cats, frequently they will say to me, "Hey, stop that, wait a minute" by hitting me with their claws when their patience is running out. They do not scratch or harm me in any way. They are simply making a strong statement. I know that "claws out," in this case, means that I have not listened when they tried to tell me with a meow or a wiggle. Cats are polite, they give a warning before they hurt you. If you declaw cats, you have taken away from them this means of being polite and giving warning first. In a way it could be likened to removing a person's larynx. Even if you promise that that person would always be protected, certainly never have to cry for help; even if you promise that that person would always have anything and everything that he or she might desire (and in real life you can never be sure you can fulfill such promises), still, the larynx is gone. The choice of communicating in the normal way is no longer that person's choice.

If you are still unsure about the question of declawing, see the chapter by Dr. Paul Rowan, "You Can't Declaw with Love," in the book *Cats Prefer It This Way,* by Carole Wilbourn and Dr. Paul Rowan, (New York: Berkley Publishing, 1977).

"Neuter and Spay, It's the Kindest Way"

"Neuter and spay, it's the kindest way" is the slogan of one of our finest humane animal organizations—Pet Pride. It certainly is the kindest and the easiest path to take for both the cat and the owner as well as for society at large. I've heard many myths about the disadvantages of neutering and spaying. People think their cats will become fat or lethargic, or will miss having a sexual life, or the female will miss mothering kittens. None of these things is true. Cats become obese and/or lethargic because of faulty feeding whether they are neutered or not. Cats live in the present—in the absolute "now"—and they become sexually stimulated and crave a mate only if their glands tell them to. Sexual thoughts or the need to mother never occur to a neutered cat. However, there *are* drawbacks for both the male and the female if they are *not* neutered.

Undesirable Behavior of the Unneutered Male Cat

Unaltered males are not kept as pets. Catteries who maintain an unaltered tom to sire kittens have anywhere from six to twenty females for him to service plus a book of outside females who come to him regularly for stud service. A male who is not used for stud regularly becomes very tense, nervous, and out of sorts, because he is uncomfortable.

Unaltered males spray. Their urine smells very strong and quite different from the urine of a neutered male. A full tom will spray in various places all around the territory that he considers his own. This is as natural as sneezing and not something he can be trained away from. Once you've smelled the urine or spray of an unaltered tom, it's not something you'll easily forget. I can tell the minute I walk into a home if somebody is keeping an unaltered tom.

If an owner lets the tom wander about the neighborhood, wander is just what he does, ranging far and wide searching for a female in heat. And when he finds one there are bound to be other toms on the spot waiting to contest his right to mate with her. There are always fights before mating. And these fights are brutal and deadly serious. A fight to the death is common; anything less is an exception. The unaltered tom, allowed to roam free, leads a short and violent life. And if there are no females in season about for a couple of weeks, his aggression will be easily triggered at home. If he becomes unaccountably rough in play, the lack of a female may be the reason why.

Undesirable Behavior of the Unspayed Female Cat

A female in heat does not spray—she calls. You can tell if a female is in season even if she doesn't call very much by stroking down her back. She will push her hindquarters up into the air with her tail looped over to the side in the final mating position. Unspayed female cats generally become high-strung, nervous, and jumpy. They are usually thin and debilitated. Going through heat after heat drains their body. They easily fall victim to any disease germ that happens to be around—their resistance is very low.

The female's ovaries manufacture eggs with each heat. Unlike humans, these eggs are not released and passed out of the body, but remain there unless the cat is fertilized. If the cat goes through heat after heat and is not fertilized, these unused eggs are encysted. Cystic ovaries are a sign of a female who has gone through several heats before she's spayed. If a cat comes into heat more than twice a year, you can be pretty sure she has cystic ovaries.

I've met a few owners who've bought male and female cats, planning to breed them. Besides all the potential problems that can be encountered in the course of the mating and birth process, having kittens is a lot of work and costs money too. The mother needs special food and extra vitamins at frequent intervals. And the kittens need constant supervision and feedings six times a day from four weeks on. Both the mother and the kittens can fall prey to a number of diseases along the way. I have warned several owners who had this idea in mind that a female can have her neck broken during mating—it is a rough and violent ritual. Also, if the mother is at all small, you could easily lose her during the birth of the kittens. Veterinarians are finding that the need for cesarean-section births are becoming more and more frequent. This is especially true with Persians, who are bred with small hips and large heads. But even a seemingly robust domestic short-haired cat can have a problem giving birth. I clearly remember my shock on seeing not one but three females in Dr. Perper's clinic one day, all cesarean cases. They would have died if the owners hadn't acted quickly and brought them in. Of these cases, not one was a Persian.

Another potential problem after the birth is that during the nursing weeks the mother may experience calcium-deficiency fits because, even if she is eating plenty of calcium-rich foods, the calcium may not be assimilated by her body.

The Nightmare of Unwanted Kittens

The wandering tom is capable of siring hundreds of kittens every year. The horror of the situation in New York City alone is something that I would rather not bring into my conscious mind. But here again, like the true facts about declawing, I think this is something that responsible people must be made aware of before they can make an intelligent decision concerning neutering, spaying, and allowing cats to have kittens.

Every single day in New York City, hundreds of cats are destroyed. The overpopulation makes cats into trash—refuse. Cats for laboratory use are in such plentiful supply that the going rate is $5 a head. There are too many kittens. Sometimes I hear, "Oh, I have homes already for my cat's kittens, even if she has ten kittens there are people just waiting to take them." I explain to these people that this means there are ten homes that could have saved the lives of ten other kittens who are already alive and otherwise will probably die horribly. Or I hear, "I just want her to have one litter." Well, let's suppose one litter results in five kittens. And let's suppose that each kitten lives fifteen years. Because you have made the decision to allow your cat to have these little mites, it behooves you to realize that each little mite represents not only six weeks of cuteness romping around your kitchen but fifteen years of life for which you and you alone are responsible.

You may blithely state that you already have five homes—five people panting to sweep a kitten up in their arms and cherish it forever. I assure you that you cannot take for granted that "forever" really *means* forever or that the new owners won't feed a poor-quality diet or leave food available between meals or leave a window open or allow the cats to run outside unsupervised. Can you be sure the cats will have a yearly exam and shots for fifteen years? Will their teeth be kept clean? And suppose, just suppose, that even one of those five kittens is not neutered and brings forth five more kittens. That's your responsibility too. If not for your original litter, the second litter would certainly never have been born. And how would you feel if one day you found out that one of those little kittens of yours had been cruelly mutilated by a declawing operation?

Neuter and spay, it's the kindest way. Suggest to your friends who want kittens that they save a cat from possible death at one of the shelters.

The Proper Time to Get Your Cat Neutered or Spayed

The very best time to have the cat neutered is, for a female, after she goes through her first heat; for a male, when the urine changes odor and becomes very pungent. These are the signs in the male and female that the sexual center has transferred from the organs to the base of the brain. You can then remove the organs and yet not disturb the basic sexuality of the cat. Insist that your cat pass through these physical changes before the operation is done. The age range can vary. I've known females to go into heat as early as six months, and I've met Persians who have shown no sign of maturity until a year and a half. The age is somewhere within that range for males also.

The operation for females is simple surgery. Because it's one of the most frequently done operations, almost any veterinarian is competent at it. Since anesthetic is used, don't forget to give the cat 500 units of vitamin C a day for two days before the operation is done (see Chapter 7).

The female stays overnight in the hospital, and when you pick her up the next day, you will be told to keep her quiet for a day or two. However, I remember when I was working for Dr. Rowan we frequently had owners telephoning all upset because their cat didn't *want* to be quiet— she didn't realize that she'd just had an operation. She felt perfectly fine and was leaping off the top of the bookcase and bounding from sofas to chairs as usual. When this operation is done by any competent veterinarian, it's a piece of cake.

Neutering a male is even easier. In fact, it's even easier than having the teeth cleaned. When Big Purr was neutered, I took him in in the morning and picked him up that evening. He didn't look any different at all, because the vet removes the testes but leaves the scrotum. He certainly didn't act any different, either. Except, thank heavens, he was no longer interested in spraying the drapes. I remember at one point I scooped him up in my arms for some reason and suddenly realized that I had lifted him with my hand under his testicles. All his weight was sitting on that recent surgery. But Purr did not have the slightest reaction; he hadn't thought a thing about it. I was all upset over nothing.

Purr still enjoys sexual play. Once I was cat sitting for a kitten who came into season while her owner was gone. She had a torrid affair with Purr day and night for a week. Purr wasn't too sure at first what he was supposed to do but after a day of experimentation, trial and error, the two of them worked it out very nicely. And my friend Phyllis' cats Barnaby and Tulip were neutered in their youth but are a completely devoted couple and enjoy sexual play on a regular basis.

Neutered cats do not suffer the terrific stress of unneutered cats. Their resistance to disease is higher; they're more mellow and happier because life is easier. They indulge in sex play because they want to, not because they are driven to it by their glands.

Grooming

Grooming not only is a necessity for our loving feline friends who live indoors, but it also establishes a wonderful and lasting bond between you and your cat. In addition to serving an important function, it is your way of expressing affection—and the purrs that greet your ears will confirm your cat's delight.

Among cats mutual grooming is a form of communication—sometimes an expression of love and companionship. Grooming is a very natural thing to the cat and something they readily understand if properly approached and properly done.

Grooming is also a necessary part of cat care. Dry, artificial heat in winter causes cats to shed excessively. Cats also shed naturally in the spring and, to a slightly less degree, again in the fall.

Cats also shed during the slightest stress situation. If you're away for a while, if you take cats to the vet, if you take them visiting, if workers come to the house, if the cats fall ill—all these are stress situations that will produce excess shedding. If the cats are not groomed regularly, with a bit of special attention during these stress times, cats will attempt to groom themselves, with the result that they will swallow a great deal of hair. Living in the wild, they would not have had to deal with many of those stress situations or with the unnatural heat. The spring and fall sheds would be the only bad times.

Swallowing a lot of excess hair can affect cats in two ways—either they will form hair balls, which they will then vomit (like miniature wet hot dogs on the carpet), or they will try to pass the hair through the intestines. Because this latter method of disposal is not the most efficient, these hair masses are frequently not passed out of the cats' bodies but lodge in curves and bends of the intestinal tract, causing blockage. Cats with this problem then stop eating—or sometimes vomit an innocuous foamy substance instead of the hair they are trying to get rid of because the hair has passed beyond the stomach and is unreachable. A veterinarian sometimes gives feline laxative in a tube, in hopes of dislodging these lower-intestinal hair masses. If that doesn't work, the doctor can try an enema and, in extreme cases, surgery. What a pity this is, when just sixty seconds of grooming a day will prevent the necessity for even the laxative.

High-Quality Diet = High-Quality Coat

If you remember why we remove food between meals (see Chapter 2, "Diet"), you'll recall that leaving it available slows down the metabolism so that wastes build up and back up. The body tries to deal with the situation by pushing some of these waste products out through the pores of the skin, resulting in oiliness and dandruff. On a low-quality diet, the cat has more waste products to deal with. Also, the hair vitamins, mostly found in the vitamin B family, have either been destroyed in the heat processing of the cat food or are simply missing because they tend to be the more expensive ones. These quality and texture vitamins are the very ones that you are now supplying through the Vita-Mineral Mix.

Good-quality hair allows shed hair to slip out of the coat easily. Hair is retained in the coat for two reasons: (1) excessive oiliness and (2) a poor-quality coat. Oiliness is caused by a diet too high in organ meats or other rich food or simply by not removing all food between meals. The lecithin in the Vita-Mineral Mix emulsifies the oil and fat and turns it into a water-soluble substance that the blood can carry off and dispose of in the urine. Oiliness turns your cats into little walking dust mops, attracting and holding not only their own hair but any dust and debris from the floor. Unwholesome hair texture works in exactly the same way. Each hair has many microscopic hairs growing out from it. On good-quality hair, these microscopic secondary hairs all grow down, pointing toward the tip of the hair and allowing dust, oil, water, and shed hair to slip right off. On poor-quality hair, they protrude out and up and every which way so they hold the dust and shed hair in the coat. You can imagine how a cat with a good-quality coat would be much easier to groom, because dust would not cling and old shed hair would come right out and not stay behind to build up into a mat in the cat's coat. The yeast, wheat germ, and kelp in the Vita-Mineral Mix are specifically for the improvement of hair quality.

The first two or three years that I was grooming, I made it a point once a year to go to a cat show. I didn't look just at the cats, because I was anxious to learn anything I could from any source available. I took note of what kind of carrying cases were used, what grooming tools, and what was in the bottles and boxes lined up on the shelf near each cat's cage. The first thing I noticed was that about 90 percent of the owners showing cats were using exactly the same bottles and boxes as all the rest. And what was in them? They were marked "Hair thickener," "Baldness preventative," "Texturing lotion," and "Whitening powder" (or "Darkening powder"). Next to these preparations, I always saw a supply of dry or semimoist cat food.

There must have been hundreds of owners there, and it amazes me to this day that evidently none of them ever made a connection between what they were feeding the cats and the need for all of those artificial cosmetics to cover up the faults in less-than-perfect coats. I have never used any sort of cosmetic powder or spray on a cat to change the existing texture of the natural coat. Such things always make the coat more prone to pick up dirt, and therefore the cat needs bathing all the more frequently. Besides, all of these preparations contain chemicals, perfumes, and the like. I will not be a party to putting such preparations on the cat when I know the cat is going to lick them off and ingest them. Virgin hair stays clean the longest. Even if the texture and thickness has not yet reached the optimum, you can't improve on nature. Hair in its natural, virgin state is uncoated, unconditioned, uncolored, and untreated. It provides the best insulation against both heat and cold. And nothing is easier for an owner to groom than virgin hair. Improve the texture, thickness, and quality of the hair by feeding the diet discussed in Chapter 2.

Finding a Groomer

New clients frequently tell me how they searched for months trying to find someone reputable and gentle to groom their cat. I must say I had the same problem, searching in vain for someone whom I could recommend to take my overload during the busy season. Even in a major metropolis like New York, I have not been able to find anyone who I would trust to groom a cat except myself and the people I train. I've looked everywhere—in pet shops, dog-grooming salons (even the most expensive), kennels, and several veterinarians' offices. What I found was that in all of those categories people with the highest standards were unwilling to groom cats because they did not feel at home doing it. They were comfortable with dogs but not with cats. People with lower standards would give it a try but were both slip-shod and rough. Veterinarians would rather spend their time curing disease than grooming, and the good ones are generally already overbooked with more serious problems.

Most veterinarians use anesthetic and/or tranquilizers before grooming. Anesthetics and tranquilizers constitute a serious stress. I found without exception that reputable veterinarians try to avoid anesthetizing and shaving a cat whenever they can. Several veterinarians I know refer all grooming problems to me.

If the local dog groomer agrees to groom your cat, I strongly advise that you arrange to be present the entire time for at least the first few visits. It is illegal for anyone but a veterinarian to dispense tranquilizers to an animal, yet I know of several groomers who slip them to cats. I have also heard all too frequently of how cats are "subdued" by dog groomers— by trusses, straps, and harnesses, or "It took three of us to hold her down." Cats can die of shock or heart attack under such brutal handling. You must be sure that anyone who grooms your cat is working *with*, not against, the cat.

If there's a problem finding someone to groom a badly matted cat or a cat with fleas or what-have-you here in the middle of New York City, I can well imagine the plight of someone living in a small town or rural area where even a dog groomer is not to be found and the only veterinarians available are those specializing in dairy herds. I decided to write this chapter in as much detail as possible for those owners who have no choice but to try their best by themselves. It is much easier if you have someone to assist you. Your assistant can distract the cat with pleasurable sensations such as throat stroking, back scratching, and murmured praise. I use the owner for this but you can get your cat's second most favorite person after yourself to help you.

I will try to give you all the help I can. Just remember that patience is the watchword. I was the slowest groomer on God's green earth when I started, but I was also the most careful.

Please be aware that just because I am telling you *how* to handle these problems does not mean that I am advising you to do so. If there's no one else, then you can give it a try. But there are many instances where I would strongly advise having the veterinarian anesthetize the cat and shave the mats out just one time. Then you can take over and maintain the coat so that it never gets matted again. Using scissors to cut through mats is dangerous business. The cat's skin texture is like the finest silk. The fact that it is loose, coupled with the bony structure and intricate musculature of the body, make it very difficult for an untutored person to safely clip mats. And, yes, they must be clipped. Using a comb on a mat is hopeless. It doesn't do any good at all. It does a lot of harm because you'll hurt the cat and teach him to hate being groomed.

If you elect to have the veterinarian shave the mats out, the perfect time would be when the teeth are cleaned. In fact, any time the cat has to be anesthetized for any reason be sure to check for tartar on the teeth and matting in the furs so these two things can get a free ride, as it were, and be taken care of then. Ear flushing is also a good thing to slip in at that time if the cat has a lot of wax in the ears, and expressing the anal glands is another item to include.

Daily Grooming

Once the cat is in good shape, you can do a complete daily grooming in sixty seconds. And daily is what it should be if you own a long-haired cat and if you're going to keep a couple of jumps ahead of the mats so that never again will your cat have to be anesthetized and shaved.

Grooming should be a pleasure for all concerned. Because you know how much cats like ritual and sameness, make grooming into a ritual. Use the same place, the same tools, and groom the cat's body parts in the same order. If possible, do the grooming at the same hour of the day. Invite the cat to the grooming area with the same signal, and always follow grooming with the same treat.

First we'll cover the grooming area. You know how sensitive your cats are to your vibrations. They sympathize when you're sick or upset. They sense your calmness when they are upset, and thus they can be calmed. Likewise, they will sense your pleasure in grooming them. So you must choose a grooming area that is pleasing to you.

I'm rather tall, so when I go into someone's home to groom their cat I always work on the kitchen counter. Also, kitchens are usually well lit,

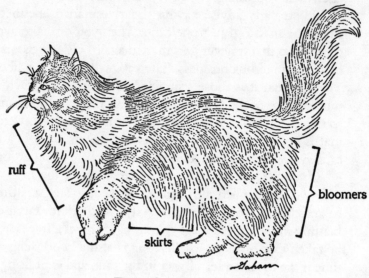

Figure 1
Ruff, skirts, and bloomers.

and that's important for the grooming area. My assistant Louise, who is only five feet tall, prefers to use something like a card table, which is a lot lower than the kitchen counter.

I do not spread a towel or anything else under the cat, because the hair sticks to it and it gets all messed up and wrinkled the minute the cat moves around, creating an uncomfortable, lumpy surface for the cat to stand on—and we want the cat to be comfortable. The surface should be clean—no sense in getting jelly on the cat's tail. After washing the surface with a sponge, be sure to dry it thoroughly with a paper towel. Standing on a damp, cold surface is not your cat's idea of comfort.

Lay out all the grooming tools. (Grooming tools will be covered later in this chapter.) When everything is set up to your satisfaction, invite your cat to the grooming.

Now, in the beginning you will be lifting the cat onto the grooming area. As time goes on and the ritual is repeated, a surprisingly large number of cats will jump the gun and leap spontaneously onto the table themselves. I've had this experience with clients that I see regularly once a month. Especially in multiple-cat households, I frequently have to deal with a "me first" problem.

It's even more important, though, that you be the one to put the cat back on the floor when you're finished. Never, never let the cat jump down. You must establish as an integral part of this ritual that you are the one who says when it is over. Telling him, "OK, you're done" and letting him jump down is simply not clear enough. You must physically pick him up and place him on the floor yourself, with words of praise and admiration.

If you are just beginning to condition the cat to the joy and comfort of being groomed, you may find it best to spend the first four or five sessions going no further than the first step or two in the grooming procedure. If all you do is establish in his mind that being up on that table brings pleasure, you've already done a great deal. Especially in the beginning, keep the sessions short. One minute is enough. Remember, sixty seconds a day accomplishes much more than a half hour on Saturday. If at all possible, be sure that you put the cat down on the floor *before* he wants to go down. Try to leave him wanting more. If you must cut out a difficult mat or clean soil off the bloomers or perform some other task that is not altogether pleasurable, always finish the grooming with some type of combing that he does like, such as going back and recombing the head and neck or the cheeks and throat. Your cat will teach you about his special, favorite places. Groomings always begin and end with your cat's special favorite places.

As soon as I get to know a cat—sometimes after five minutes, sometimes after five months—I use my face and mouth a lot while grooming. Because cats groom with their mouths, they seem to understand and enjoy having me kiss them on the top of their heads and murmur; take their ears between my lips and, as it were, "hug them with my mouth"; and breathe warm air against the skin at the back of the neck or the shoulders. With a nervous cat, putting your face close to the cat's head or body gives him confidence, because subconsciously he knows that your face and eyes are vulnerable and that you would not expose them so if there were any reason to get upset. Because you do expose your face and eyes so casually, the cat thinks that everything must be all right.

A word of caution: Be careful not to puff air into the ears, eyes, or nose. Cats won't like that a bit. And, instead of the calming effect you're trying for, they'll struggle to get away from that unpleasant sensation. Also, do not accompany your kisses with a loud kissing sound, especially not near the cat's ear. This sound is extremely piercing, even for a human. And for a cat a kissing sound at the ear opening is quite painful.

You can try using classical music while you groom, as an additional part of the ritual. A record or tape is best, because then you have control of what is being played. It should be played rather softly and be either soothing or happy. The main requirement is that you personally enjoy it. Steer clear of jazz, rock, or pop music. The latest scientific experiments indicate that plants and animals respond best to classical or religious music; Bach and Ravi Shankar have the most positive effect.

When you use a shaver, the cat must be anesthetized because a shaver is painful. There are several other grooming tools for sale to the professional groomer that make one think of a medieval torture chamber. One is called "the mat splitter." Having a mat splitter sounded like such a terrific idea that I ordered one. When the thing came, I was absolutely aghast at its design. It was something like a rake with curved teeth sharpened like little razors. I assume one is expected to drag it through the mats, incorporating some sort of sawing motion in the process. I could see at once that it was totally impractical and so badly designed as to be dangerous. I tried very gently running it through the silky fur of a freshly groomed cat. Even those lovely unmatted hairs were caught and pulled on the curved blades. I didn't even finish the stroke but threw the sadistic tool into the wastebasket. Over the years, I've run into many strange grooming tools that owners pull out of drawers to show me what they have been using to groom their cats. Any time an owner tells me his or her cat "hates being groomed," I always ask to see the grooming tool. There's one sure way to make it clear to owners that a tool hurts: I hand them the tool and ask them to run it through their own hair.

The Grooming Tools

You will have to be the judge of what tool a cat's coat needs. Here is a list of the tools I carry around with me and their purpose (Illustration 2):

- Nail clipper (the best kind are people toenail clippers), to clip the claws
- Q-tips, for cleaning ears
- Vitamin E capsules (100-unit), for oiling Q-tips
- Resco professional combs, fine, medium, and coarse
- Spratt superfine comb, for "crew-cut" on Persians or all over for short-haired cats

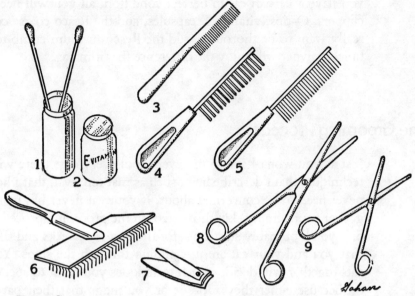

Figure 2

Grooming tools

1. cotton swabs
2. 100 unit vitamin E capsules
3. superfine metal comb
4. coarse metal comb

5. medium coarse metal comb
6. Twinco Slicker Brush—small
7. human toenail clipper
8. and 9. round nosed surgical scissors.

- Blunt-nosed surgical scissors (available from surgical supply house), for cutting through mats
- Twinco slicker brush (size small), *for short-haired cats only*

Most combs available in pet shops look like a human comb made out of metal, with a thicker tooth at each end. They don't work well because those end teeth catch and pull the cat's fur. They are also usually poor-quality metal, which again causes the comb to catch in the fur. The Resco professional combs are good-quality metal and are medium priced. You can try calling pet shops to see if they stock them, or perhaps they can order them for you. I order them through the mail.

The preceding list is almost a full grooming kit for a professional cat groomer. For everyday grooming on a short-haired cat who is in good condition, all you need is the nail clippers, Q-tips, vitamin E capsules, and slicker brush. An outlay of about $5 will probably cover the lot. If you have a Persian cat in perfect condition, all you will need is the nail clippers, Q-tips, vitamin E capsules, and the Resco coarse comb. If you really want to be thorough, add the Resco medium comb to the list. A finicky owner will enjoy the difference that it makes.

The Grooming Procedure

Just as you won't have to use every tool every day, there will be several techniques that I describe here, such as mat removal, that I hope you will never need to be concerned about. If your cat never has mats or doesn't get ear wax, simply skip those steps in the grooming procedure. Just as I did, you'll probably start slow for the first few weeks and then later find that you and your cat are just gliding through the steps. You and your cats together will decide which techniques you want to spend extra time on because either they adore it or you judge that their particular coats need it.

Step 1: Finger Grooming

No matter what you're going to do in the grooming, always begin every grooming with your hands. After you place the cat on the grooming table, facing away from you, stroke his head, neck, throat, chest, back, outer thighs, stomach, inner thighs, and bloomers. The reason for this "finger grooming" is that you are demonstrating to the cat what it is you are about to do and also what a pleasant, exciting feeling it is going to be. As you stroke, think in your mind, "I'm going to make you feel good here, and I'm going to make your furs nice there. I'm going to clean out that nasty loose hair." Think of massaging the cat's muscles with your fingertips, stimulating circulation ever so lightly.

The second purpose for the "finger grooming" is to familiarize yourself with the condition of your cat's body and coat for today. Any little mats? How's the texture? Any soil on the bloomers? Has anything been dribbled onto that lovely ruff? Long before you finish your "finger grooming," you should be rewarded with a resonant purr.

Then, when you introduce the grooming tool, it will simply be an extension of what you've already done. The grooming tool will help you express the love more efficiently. Properly used, it should make your cat feel even better than your fingers did. His purr may increase in volume or be augmented by kneading with front paws.

Step 2: Light Combing

If your cat is short-haired, Step 2 applies *only* if there is a buildup of loose hair in the coat as found during the shedding seasons. Usually for a short-haired cat you can skip this step and simply use the slicker brush, described later.

If you're working with a long-haired cat and at some point on the body you encounter resistance indicating tangles or mats, go no further on that particular body area. Mats and tangles are dealt with later in Step 4, after clipping the nails.

If cats are matted, they know it, and they also know just where the mats are. They will be afraid to have you comb through the mats because they know that such combing hurts. So don't even try to comb a resistant area; instead, follow the directions given in Step 4 of the grooming procedure. On most days of the year, the whole combing procedure will be a "light combing" because you will not encounter resistance at any point—no mats and no tangles.

The first time that you decide to groom your cat seriously, by far the best plan is to begin with a comb that you think is sure to be too coarse (wide-toothed) and begin by using a stroke that you think is sure to be too light. You don't want to pull or make the cat uncomfortable in any way. If the comb goes sailing through without bringing very much hair with it, you can always graduate to the medium comb, then the fine. If you begin with a fine-toothed comb, you could end up pulling the hairs, which is uncomfortable. Or, as frequently happens, because the teeth of the comb are so close together, the comb may go slipping across the tops of the hairs, grooming them only about a quarter of the way down and leaving all the old, loose hair still lodged untouched near the roots.

Each time you begin grooming, remember to think of using the comb as a method of exploration. Don't automatically assume that the tips of the teeth are going to reach the cat's skin on the first stroke. Mentally divide the length of the cat's hair into quarters. On the first round over the cat's body, let the comb lightly explore the top quarter—the tips of the hair. If all is smooth sailing, go back over the cat again and include the next layer down, combing the outer *half* of the hairs. If you begin to encounter any resistance as the comb goes through, stop and comb that particular area even more lightly at first so that you gradually work the old hair out. Do the same on the third round, when you are combing through the outer three-quarters of the hairs, and on the fourth round, which ends with nice, firm strokes and the teeth scratching the skin.

You need two hands to comb a cat. Your comb hand grips the comb right up by the teeth, with your thumb actually resting against one side of the teeth, near the shank. You must use slow strokes while you're learning because your thumb must learn to be a sensory organ. It is through your thumb that you first get the message if there is any tangling or resistance to the stroke. In other words, the sensitivity of your thumb keeps your cat safe from pulling.

Your other hand is used to smooth the skin flat ahead of the comb stroke. A healthy cat's skin is quite loose and can form rolls or rumples under the fur. So this second hand is the "stroking hand." The reason for using the stroking hand will be easier to understand if you realize that, although we want to comb all the cat's fur, some of that fur is located over protruding bones such as those found by the armpit or just in front of the tail.

As I said before, a healthy cat has loose skin. So the stroking hand is used to shift that loose skin about so that you can move the fur away from the bone or hollow and comb through it easily—then let it go back in place. You will probably find it helpful to practice sliding your cat's skin around. It feels awfully good, like any good massage, and can be incorporated into your usual petting and fondling routine.

Explain to the cat what you are doing as you work and be very clear about the reasons for each move you make. "This will get rid of the nasty dirt on your beautiful ruff." Or "You'll feel so much better when all that old, loose hair is gone."

If, during the course of the grooming your cat makes a complaint or gives an alarm, *don't ignore it! Stop.* Nothing makes a cat more nervous than to think that he has no control over the situation. If he tells you to stop, stop. Acknowledge that you have heard. Try to find out what the problem is. Carefully solve the problem, explaining all the while how you intend to do it without hurting. Then continue on. Remember that the whole grooming is one big expression of affection.

Here is the order in which you do the combing:

First, start with the back of the neck—they all love that.

Second, then go on to the throat and chest. The cat should be seated, facing away from you. Reach the comb hand around one side of him and the stroking hand around the other side. Tip the cat's head back slightly and, starting at the top, on the cheeks, stroke the comb downward (Illustration 3), using slow and short strokes. Work your way down gradually. No stroke should be longer than three or four inches. Remember, you're still exploring. Overlap your strokes so that each stroke is *begun* in an area that has already been combed and ends by stroking through uncombed hair. Work your way down from the cheeks through the throat, upper chest, and lower chest, reaching between the legs. Your "finger grooming" will have revealed to you the bone structure under that chest fur so that you can avoid bumping the hard comb teeth against any protruding bones.

Third, comb the neck or throat again—not because it needs it, but because cats love it and you want to reinforce the feeling of pleasure at being groomed. For this reason, you'll be going back to the neck and throat after finishing each section of the cat's body.

Figure 3
To comb the ruff, tip the cat's head back slightly.

Fourth, do the back. Remember the little bumpy bones you found in the chest area? Well, you now have a whole long spine of bones running down the back. A good way to keep an area safe from the comb is to put your finger over the area. So put a finger over the upper spine and think of your cat's back as being shaped like the roof of a house with the spine on top. Comb one side and then the other, stroking parallel to the spine but never allowing the comb to go bumping down the vertebrae. The back is where you will learn how to use the stroking hand. There are three ways to use the stroking hand, depending on which area you are working on and/or the texture of your cat's hair and skin. The first method is to move the stroking hand ahead of the comb, pulling the skin forward and making sure there are no protruding bones or muscles for the comb to hit against (Illustration 4) and hurt the cat. The second method

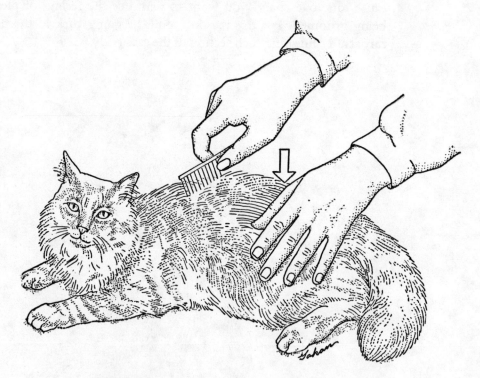

Figure 4

First stroking hand method—
The skin is stretched by applying pressure with the underside of the base of the thumb (at arrow).

Figure 5

Second stroking hand method—
The skin is held taut behind the comb, again using
the underside of the base of the thumb
to apply pressure (see arrow).

is to use the stroking hand to hold the skin taut *behind* the comb, using the thumb to press the skin backward (Illustration 5). A variation of this is using the thumb of the stroking hand to press or pull the skin to one side or the other in order to move it off a protruding bone or inaccessible depression in the cat's body. If all this sounds complicated, just remember the purpose of the stroking hand, which is to keep the comb or brush from hitting against the cat's sensitive bones and to smooth out skin rumples.

When combing the back, as in combing the throat, use short strokes. Once you've become thoroughly familiar with your cat's body structure, you will know how many bumps and depressions lurk between the neck and the tail. Comb the back hair a little at a time, and use the same overlap technique that you used on the neck. Also, remember that the stroking hand is being used to control the tautness of the skin, and you will soon discover that that control cannot extend for more than three or four inches from the hand's position.

A word about the comb angle: The comb should be held at a right angle to the cat's body. The points of the comb teeth should be directed against the skin. Don't think of combing hair, think of scratching skin.

In training a new client to comb his or her cat between groomings, I find that the most frequent mistake is to angle the teeth of the comb forward so that you are pushing the pointy teeth through the hair. This way your thumb cannot feel any sudden tangling, nor are you getting the teeth down to the skin. The second most frequent, and by far the worst, mistake is what I call the "egg-beater technique." Here, not only is the comb angled with the teeth pointing forward but the wrist is flipped at the end of each stroke causing the comb to lift or pull the hair out away from the body. Instead of starting at the tip of the hair and working down to the root layer by layer, egg-beater aficionados dig in as close to the root as possible and attempt to lift or pull *all* the loose hair off the cat at once. The thought in their minds seems to be that they are trying to comb and fluff the cat at the same time. They usually compound the error by using quick, flipping strokes, which reminds me of someone beating an egg with a fork—hence my label, "egg-beater technique." (Obviously, this mistake is almost never made by owners of short-haired cats.) I explain to them that no one can fluff the cats' coats better than the cats themselves, when they shake vigorously after the grooming is over. And the very best way to ensure that your cats will want to have a good shake is to slick their hair down, then just let them go.

Fifth, do the thighs. By now it has become obvious that skin that is stretched taut is easiest to comb over. You've used the stroking hand to accomplish this on the back. For the thigh, there is a third stroking hand technique you can use. Simply place your stroking hand under the cat's belly, and slowly and gently begin lifting upward ever so slightly. Watch the thigh, leg, and foot. As you lift, the cat will automatically stretch the leg out, reaching for the table (Illustration 6). While the leg is stretched thus, take advantage. Now it's a simple matter to do your light, medium, and heavy stroke combing, stroking from the top of the thigh down. When I do this area, I always have the cat facing sideways. I reach in from the back and lift up. This is a perfect position for combing the bloomers, too, because the back of the leg is stretched out as well as the side.

Now, instead of turning the cat around at this point to do the other outer thigh, leave the cat where he or she is and do the inner thigh of the *opposite* leg. Again, with the stroking hand slip the hand underneath the

Figure 6
Lift up on abdomen to stretch
outer thigh for combing.

foot of the leg you were just stretching and gently press up so that the foot and leg fold up against the side of the abdomen. The cat is now standing on three legs (Illustration 7). Bend over the cat, look underneath, past the abdomen, and you will see the inner thigh of the opposite leg. Reach under with the comb past the leg you are holding up, and comb out that inner thigh. (At this point, you will find yourself in a position that looks a lot more difficult and impressive than it really is.)

Here I'd better say a word about the tail. In order for cats to stand still and cooperate with you, they must control an awful lot of energy and nervous impulses. Most cats really do a terrific job. They are awe inspir-

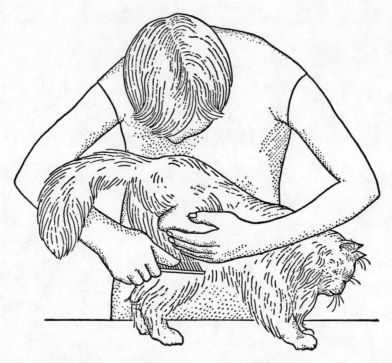

Figure 7
To comb the inner thigh, slip the stroking hand under the outside
foot and gently lift it up. DON'T LIFT TOO HIGH because your
cat must balance on three legs.

ing. One thing that enables them to accomplish this is that they can vent
a lot of energy and nervousness with their tails: They can flick them, lash
them from side to side, and generally express all the feelings they would
otherwise have to bottle up. Owners frequently have the impulse to confine the tail or hold it still while working on bloomers, anal area, inner
thigh, and so on. I tried the same thing in the beginning while I was
learning. The cats soon made it very clear that if their tails are held still,
then the movement will have to come out somewhere else. So, if you
don't want dancing feet, you should as much as possible leave the tail free
and try to work around it.

Now, turn the cat around facing the opposite direction to do the
other thigh. Once again, lift up on the tummy to do that outer thigh and

bloomers. This time, slip the arm and hand under the cat from the front; then fold up the leg and reach under the cat to do the other inner thigh.

Sixth, the long, silky hair that forms the border between the sides of the cat and the belly is what I refer to as the "skirts." The skirts near the front of the thigh and near the armpit are areas where frequent matting occurs. Bloomers, skirts, and chest are the three areas that must be done every day.

To groom the skirts, you use somewhat the same technique as the outer thigh. Stretch out the area by lifting the cat. Face the cat away from you, open the stroking hand, and slip it under the cat's armpits and chest so that one armpit is resting on your middle finger and the other armpit is resting on your thumb. The index finger is against the cat's chest pointed up, toward his throat. Once again you are going to lift the cat, but don't lift the cat to a perpendicular position. This would make him afraid of falling backward, and he will probably start scrabbling with his back feet. Instead, this is a subtle move. Lift up just enough to disengage the front feet from the table by about two or three inches. The cat will be on a gentle diagonal, the chest resting heavily on your hand (Illustration 8). Now, instead of lifting any farther, stretch the cat a tiny bit more forward, away from you, so that the skin under the skirts is nicely stretched out and you can do light, medium, or heavy combing of the skirts. Do the chest and abdomen at the same time as you reach under the cat and around to the skirts on the other side. You can even do fronts of thighs in this position, and that very tricky place where skirts join fronts of thighs.

In the beginning, before you and your cat get used to this little piece of choreography, you will almost certainly have to put the cat down, reposition your grip, and lift again for a few more strokes. You may find it helpful to go back and comb the neck a few times between tries to reinforce positive feelings, especially when you're first learning this maneuver.

Seventh, the chest between the front legs is mostly done by what I call the *Braille method*—you can't see what you're doing. Stand the cat facing away from you on all fours and bring the stroking hand in from one side, the comb in from the other. Reaching up between the front legs as high up on the chest as you can, stroke with one hand and follow with the comb. Coming at it from the other angle, tilt the cat's chin up and comb down on the upper chest, trying to overlap with what you did on the lower chest by reaching between the legs.

Figure 8

To comb the skirts place one hand under the chest between the
legs and lift up, stretching the cat slightly forward.

Eighth, grooming the tail is left for the final comb-out. Remember to
finish by going back and combing the pleasure area again—neck, throat,
or lower spine. A special word about the tail—use only the coarse comb
on the tail no matter how sparse you think your cat's coat is. You didn't
allow the comb to bump against the spinal vertebrae, and you apply the
same principle here. The tail is an extension of the spine and very sensitive. Comb it in sections, just as you did the body of the cat. Don't try to

cover the entire tail, base to tip, in one stroke. Work down in layers as you did with the combing of the body, and be supercareful not to pull and not to dig in. Tails are delicate and sensitive.

Step 3: Clipping the Nails

Nail clipping can be made very easy if the owner remembers to always include stroking the paws whenever he or she is petting the cat. Make it a practice to massage the cat's pads and toes, massage the claws out and in, out and in, as a part of your everyday ritual of affection. That way, when it comes to claw-clipping time, the cat will not find it in any way odd or

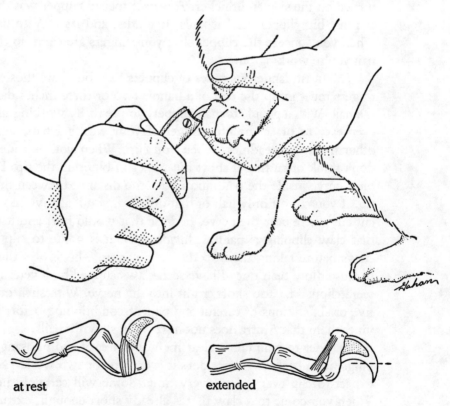

at rest   extended

Figure 9
Clip the claw parallel to the ground.
Clip only the area below dotted line.

alarming that you are picking up a paw and extruding the claws. Moreover, you must be familiar with the anatomy of your cat's claws before you try cutting them. This everyday fondling of the paws and claws gives you the opportunity you need to examine just how the claw slides in and out of the sheath. You will notice the downward curve of the claw as well as two other important features—the claw is flat (not round like a dog's claw), and there is a little pink membrane inside the claw reaching about halfway down the curve.

When I first started grooming, I experimented with every type of nail clipper I could get my hands on. I came to the conclusion that every single one I tried was designed for a small dog with a round claw. My pussycats did not have round claws; their claws are flat like my nail but turned on the side and thicker. A people toenail clipper was the answer. A great big clipper for flat nails. It works, and it's easy to use because when you squeeze the clipper shut your fingers are right up close to the nail you're working on.

The most dangerous types of clippers I've found are those where the fingers must grasp the end of a handle two or three inches distant from the nail. With a people toenail clipper, you're really working in close. It's even easy to brace the little finger of your working hand against your other hand for steadiness when you clip. When you extrude the claw, don't think of cutting it short but rather of blunting the tip. Locate that pink nerve inside the nail, and notice the distance between that and the tip. If you cut off only half of that distance, you'll always be safe. Never cut anywhere near the nerve, because that would hurt and teach the cat that claw clipping is painful. Incidentally, it is polite to clip your cats' claws before taking them to the veterinarian. This is also the best plan because more than once I have seen claws clipped by a veterinarian that were clipped far too short, right into the nerve. With such cats, it takes five or six sessions of careful and patient conditioning before I can convince them that Anitra does not hurt when she clips nails.

In order to maintain a clear memory of easy and pleasant claw clippings, it's nice if the owner does it every one or two weeks. Now, don't expect to clip every claw every time. Some will certainly not need it. When you come to a claw that is already short enough, extrude it from the sheath as usual and just touch it gently with the metal clipper so that the cat has the impression that you have done something to each claw.

A word about extruding the claws: On the first try, most people try to squeeze the claw out. This will work, but it is not efficient and certainly doesn't make the cat feel good. Instead, put your finger on the pad under the claw, press up, and watch the claw come out automatically. Use your thumb above the claw to hold the skin and hair out of the way and keep the claw from sliding back into its sheath. Look at the curve of the claw, and, as you position your clipper, think of making the clip so that the flattened end of the claw will end up parallel to the ground when the cat steps on it—not up and down and parallel to the wall in front of the cat.

Before you actually squeeze the clipper shut, make sure of two things. First and foremost, there must be no chance of catching a part of the pad in the clipper, second, hold the clipper still as you squeeze it—don't move it from side to side, change position in any way, or pull.

After you've finished grooming, the cat will probably run to the scratching post and start scratching like crazy to get his nails back in shape again the way he likes them.

Step 4: Getting Rid of the Mats

I feel a tremendous amount of hesitation in including instructions on the use of scissors for cutting out mats. It's such a dangerous business. And it's so hard to describe to someone second-hand, without having them actually present with the cat and the scissors.

I found that the very hardest cats to cut mats out of were elderly cats, because the skin is loose and flaccid as opposed to being loose and elastic; and black cats with dark skins, because it's hard to see where the hair ends and the skin begins. I remember the first matted cat I ever had to groom. It was quite an initiation. The cat was so matted that he was crippled. Any place a cat could get mats, he had them. The mats around the anus were mixed with excrement. He even had little minimats formed in the crew-cut between his ears. The rest of the body looked as if it were in a plaster cast between an inch and two inches thick. My first impulse when I saw him was to cry. I had never seen a cat in such a pitiful condition in all my life. I don't remember now what the owner's excuse was for allowing the cat to get like that, but I do remember that that first grooming of my entire life lasted five hours. I didn't know enough then to insist on stopping after two hours and coming back another day, giving the cat a rest. I know I worked slowly—I remember the owner complained about how slowly it was going. But my feelings about a human being who could allow a cat to get into that condition were such that I didn't give a damn about what that owner thought about anything. My sole concern was to help the cat.

Here are a few tried and true general rules that will help you:

1. Before you cut and as you cut, be very sure that the whole time you can see where the skin is and where the hair is. If you lose sight of the skin, don't cut—stop.

2. With every single cut you do, cut slowly. Be aware of every single millimeter of the cutting motion.

3. You don't have to finish an area before going on to the next area. Work a little here, a little there. It's easier on the cat's nerves to go back again and again to a difficult spot, doing it in short tries.

4. When working on one mat, don't hesitate to switch angles of approach—working at it from the right, from the left, from the bottom, from all angles.

5. Give frequent rest breaks. Especially when removing mats, you must remember to put the cat down off the table *before* he starts wiggling and demanding it. If you're working with scissors, the cat must be still, not wiggly. You can spread out the mat removal process over days and weeks, doing a few mats a day. Simply say to yourself that the coat is no longer getting worse and worse—it is now improving, however slowly. Safety comes first.

6. *Don't bathe the cat while mats are still in the coat.*

7. Whenever you are working near any delicate area where you are afraid of cutting something such as a nipple or penis, just remember—if you know where it is, you won't cut it. So cover such areas with your finger while you're working nearby.

8. If the cat is moving, don't cut. Stop.

Splitting the Mats. Mats pull the skin terribly, especially on areas of articulation such as knees, thighs, and armpits—they hurt. Don't pet your cat on the mats. The less you touch them or move them around, the better. As I said, they hurt.

The very first thing I do for a matted cat is to split each mat apart into smaller pieces. This accomplishes three things. First and foremost, it gives the cat relief from the constant terrible pulling. Second, it demonstrates just what it is I am about to do to make him or her feel better. Third, it lets me see where the skin is. A mat is easier to remove in pieces than left whole. When I first began training my assistant to remove mats, I advised her that if she split the mat into enough segments there would be very little else left for her to do.

To split a mat, insert the rounded nose of the lower blade of the scissors between the skin and the mat so that the scissors are perpendicular (at right angles) to the skin. In other words, the blunt side of the blade is against the skin, and the sharp cutting edge is pushing up against the mat, (Illustration 10). Caution—do not use the scissors blade to pull the mat up or away from the skin. You want the skin to stay flat and smooth, moving it as little as possible. So leave the blunt edge of the blade resting firmly on the skin and begin to *slowly* cut the mat in half.

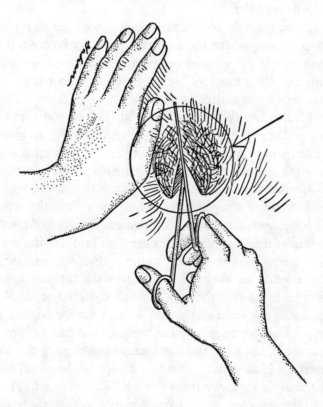

Figure 10

Splitting a mat—to split a mat hold the scissors
at a right angle to the skin.

Notice how, when the cutting in half is complete, the two halves of the mat spring apart. This is evidence that you have just released a great deal of tension from the skin.

Split the same mat again and again. Try inserting the scissors between skin and mat from various angles. You will notice that with each mat certain angles are fairly easy, while other angles of entry are all but impossible. You just hurt the cat if you insist on fighting the lay of the hair. This splitting procedure so far is fairly safe as long as you never pull the mat up away from the body. Simply keep the cutting edge facing up away from the cat and cut through the mat. In other words, you are not removing the mat, you are splitting it into many small pieces. Do this with several, if not all, of the mats wherever they occur. Split them up to give the cat relief.

Some mats do not lend themselves well to this type of splitting. With armpit mats, where the anatomy is so convoluted, it is extremely difficult to slip the scissors between skin and mat. Also, mats around the anus and the bloomers are sometimes cement hard because they have been repeatedly soiled.

Cutting Out the Pieces of the Mat. Just as you slipped the scissors between skin and mat and tilted the cutting edge up away from the cat to split the mat, to cut out pieces of the mat you must slip the blade in between the cat and the mat and tilt the blade before cutting.

Choose a piece of mat. Note where the mat is, where the skin is, and the little bit of straight hair holding the mat to the skin. Slip the scissors blade between the mat and skin *close to the edge of the mat*. In other words, instead of inserting the blade near the middle of the mat to split it, insert the blade as close as possible to the edge of the mat. Begin tilting the cutting edge of the blade up, away from the cat, just as you did when you were going to split the mat. This time, however, don't tilt it all the way up. Bring it almost all the way so that the flat edge of the blade is on an angle. Then again slowly cut through the hair between mat and skin at that angle, releasing the few hairs at the edge of the piece of mat. Then insert the blade again, close to the edge of the piece, tilt the cutting edge of the blade up away from the cat (but not to a full ninety degrees) and cut through a few more hairs, separating even more of the piece of mat from the cat. Repeat this process until you have severed all the hairs that are holding the piece of mat to the body. This technique is also used on mats that are too thick or hard to split or mats that are in difficult anatomical areas where it would be dangerous to try to split them (armpits, elbows, and ankles).

I cannot say it often enough—go slowly. The slower you go in the beginning, the better a groomer you will be in the end. The cat must be standing still, for his or her own safety, so here's a prime place to use an assistant to help keep the cat from wiggling around. A general suggestion: When you are inserting the scissors blade near the edge of the mat, the closer to the edge the better. In other words, the fewer hairs you try to snip through at one time, the safer you will be. Once again, it's a question of patience on your part. If the matting is extensive, it's far better to have the cat anesthetized and shaved that one time if you can trust the veterinarian.

Breaking Up Soft Mats: A soft mat is a mat that is not really a mat yet. Think of a cotton ball. It's nice and soft; it's not a bit lumpy—yet you could not comb through a cotton ball. If, during the light combing, you encounter any areas on the cat's coat where the comb will not go through but you can't feel a lump, treat it as a soft mat. If you do nothing about it, it will soon become a classic hard mat. Treat the soft mat exactly the same as when splitting a mat, except that in this case, to save as much hair as possible, you should slip in your scissors parallel to the lay of the hair and then cut parallel to the lay of the hair. Don't cut across the lay, thus cutting off a lot of hair. Only cut through the tangles and debris that crisscross back and forth across the growing hair. The effect will be as if you were thinning. Cut parallel to the lay of the hair again and again and again, always keeping the cutting surface facing out away from the cat, just as you did in splitting the mat. Then take the comb and, beginning with a very light touch, gradually work deeper and deeper toward the skin, removing the hairy debris you have freed.

Step 5A: For Long-haired Cats: The Final Comb-Out

This step is simply a repetition of Step 2—light combing. It is always done after removing mats or breaking up soft mats. This step ends when you're combing through the entire cat with the points of the comb tines stroking directly against the skin of the cat and when you are encountering no resistance whatsoever in any part of the cat's fur.

Use a coarse comb for this step. Then, if your cat's fur is not very thick, you can repeat with the medium comb and maybe even follow that with the fine comb, but only on crew-cut cheeks, neck, and throat—places where it doesn't pull at all. The work with the medium and fine combs is for the pleasure of finicky owners and their fortunate cats. The purr crescendos to fortissimo during this step.

Step 5B: For Short-Haired Cats: The Slicker Brush

The slicker brush is a delightful tool that short-haired cats become very fond of. Because it only reaches from one-half to three-quarters of an inch of hair, it is unsuitable for long-haired cats. If your cat has long hair, a slicker brush would groom only the tips of the hair. The slicker brush must be used properly, because it can prick and cut if improperly handled. Use the slicker brush only on the back, the sides, outer thighs, throat, and chest. Do not use it on the stomach—it could injure the nipples.

Hold the slicker brush very loosely by the handle and stroke it ever so lightly down the cat's coat. The cats often press up against the slicker brush, urging you on to a firmer stroke. Let your cat guide you. In order to avoid pricking the cat with those sharp little needles of metal, be sure that you always keep the handle low and close to the cat's body. When learning to use a slicker brush, beginners always make the same two mistakes: They try to stroke too rapidly and, worse, they flick their wrist at the end of the stroke, thus raising the handle up and digging the little wires into the cat's skin. The first two or three days that you try it, make each stroke an individual activity (Illustration 11).

It's helpful to stroke the slicker brush a couple of times down your own forearm. Try it very lightly—a feather touch. Then add a little steady pressure. This will go a long way toward helping you to know your tool. Now try this: Stroking in slow motion, begin to raise the handle up away from your arm at the end of the stroke. Do it slowly, because you will feel how those little prickles dig in to the skin. A good way to keep the wire bristles at the right angle is to think of keeping the back of the brush flat and parallel to the skin surface that you are brushing.

Some groomers hesitate to recommend the slicker brush for fear the client will use it carelessly and condition the cat to dislike being groomed because of the pain experienced from tipping the brush at an improper angle at the end of the stroke. But nothing works as well as a Twinco slicker brush for short-haired cats. Nothing removes the loose hair quite so efficiently and in such great volumes. Nothing scratches and stimulates the cat's skin in quite so delightful a fashion. Cats have told me with

Figure 11
Slicker brush—for short haired cats only. Stroke down the back
parallel to the spine keeping the handle low and close to the
body.

their purrs and by pressing their bodies up against the brush that they
adore it when it's used right.

Now, this is a cheap tool, and you will have to replace it every year or
less. If the little wires get out of line, they hurt. But I haven't found another brand that the cats like so well or that gets the loose hair out quite
so efficiently as the Twinco slicker brush (size small).

Because you can't use the slicker brush on the abdomen or any bony
place, such as the forelegs or tail, use the fine-tooth comb for those areas.
Never press hard against the bones or the tail. Remember, the tail is an
extension of the spine.

Step 6: Cleaning the Eyes

Many Persian cats have a congenital weakness in the tear ducts because of heedless breeding to get the "pushed-in-face look" (they call it the Peke face, as in Pekinese dogs), leaving insufficient room for the tear ducts. The same problem can be encountered in careless breeding of Siamese for the superelongated face.

I have seen eye exudations on other cats as well. Runny-eye syndrome often markedly improves and in some cases clears up completely when the high-quality diet is implemented and all food is removed between meals. But in cases of eye infection or where careless breeding has rendered the tear ducts all but nonexistent, you do have to clean the cat's eyes every day, and sometimes twice a day.

It's easy. Read the section on giving eye medication in Chapter 7. Do everything the same way—facing the cat away from you, taking care to approach the eye from behind, using preliminary stroking in the eye area to let the cat know what you are about to do. Then instead of putting medication on your finger and wiping it off on the inside of the lower lid, just cover your finger with a couple of layers of sterile guaze. Dip it in sterile boric acid, and wipe the debris away. If you squeeze a clean drop of the boric acid solution into the eye as well, that's even better. It's best to do it every day so that the debris does not build up, because it can stain the lovely fur around the eyes, nose, and cheeks. Also, such debris holds germs—it is a body waste, and it's best removed. I have had amazing results using golden seal tea instead of boric acid. Just add one drop of golden seal extract to one teaspoonful of water and put a drop or two into each eye twice a day for a week, then three times a week for as long as needed. Eye exudations decrease by 75 to 90 percent, and redness always disappears.

Step 7: Examining Teeth and Gums

Just as you should be aware of the condition of the cat's stool and urine for your own peace of mind, you will want to keep abreast of the condition of the teeth and gums. Tartar builds up on the teeth of most cats sooner or later, and it must be removed before it compromises the health of the gums, upper respiratory system, and finally the entire organism. If you notice that the gums have a line of bright red near the teeth, this indicates that something is amiss in the cat's system. Begin the acid-alkaline diet swing, as described in Chapter 7, for two weeks if you find inflamed gums. Also, be sure the teeth are clean.

So, how are you going to look at the cat's gums? Take the pill-giving and ear- and eye-medicating position: Kneel on the floor with your knees apart and feet together behind you, and then back the cat in toward you. With your left hand, bring your thumb and forefinger under the cat's cheekbones and lift the head up, tilting it back as if to give a pill. With the right hand, lift the upper lip enough to peek at the gums and see if there's any tartar on the teeth. Then pull the lower lip down to check out the lower teeth. Also, insert the nail of your middle finger between the upper and lower front teeth and pull the lower jaw down so you can get a better look at the molars and the inside edge of the upper and lower teeth.

On your first examination, become consciously aware of the difference in color between teeth and tartar. If I find anything amiss with a cat's teeth or gums, I always show the owner. I have found that most owners can easily see the line of red on the gums near the teeth but most are not able to distinguish between tooth and tartar.

So, in the beginning, examine the cat's teeth as a part of each grooming just so you can learn what the tartar looks like. Then, after it becomes obvious to you, you need only examine the teeth once a week. If you become aware that there's an awful lot of tartar buildup, plus inflamed gums, let the veterinarian clean the teeth. (See Chapter 8, "Going to the Vet.") The gums will probably not improve until you clean the filthy tartar away from them.

Because teeth cleaning involves the use of anesthetic, hopefully this will not have to be done more than once a year at the most. Priscilla needs to have her teeth done every year, while Big Purr is eight years old and his teeth have never needed cleaning. If you see tartar forming in between cleanings, you can sometimes flick it off with a fingernail. This is easiest done if you let the tartar build up to a good-sized chunk first (a layer or two is too hard to deal with). Then one day while you're examining, instead of simply pulling the lip back and looking, insert your right thumbnail between the tartar and the gum. Place your right index finger on the point of that tooth and attempt to scrape that tartar down with the thumbnail toward the waiting index finger. This procedure is easier to practice on some cats than on others because of the cat's temperament, the owner's skill, and the density of the tartar. My Priscilla's tartar resembles granite, and the veterinarian advised me that my efforts with a thumbnail were worse than hopeless. However, I frequently use this method on cats that I'm grooming. The best approach is not to force the issue. Make a gentle attempt, each time you examine the teeth, to flick off some tartar. If the cat protests, respond politely with "OK, never mind, we'll try it again tomorrow." The cat will soon begin to smooth out your technique if you persist with patience.

However, don't try flicking tartar off the teeth if the gums are too inflamed. Inflamed gums hurt. Let the veterinarian take care of it under anesthetic.

Step 8: Cleaning the Ears

I like to do the ears last, because many cats find ear cleaning itchy and tickly, because there are many little hairs in the ear that get moved around by the Q-tip. Many cats' ears are just not dirty, and in such cases I skip the ear cleaning. But, if you see a couple of black specks of wax, just take the Q-tip and clean *any part of the ear that you can actually see.* Don't try cleaning down into the ear canal, because you need a refined technique for that. It's not uncommon for a well-meaning owner to inadvertently tamp the wax down farther into the ear canal and against the ear drum.

It's nice to put oil on the Q-tip. Mineral oil is acceptable but, because the cat is going to wash the oil off and swallow it as soon as you put him down, I prefer to use the contents of a 100-unit vitamin E capsule. The capsules are easy to carry around with me as I go grooming from house to house. I just cut the tip off a capsule, squeeze the contents onto a saucer, and roll the end of the Q-tip in it. That way I feel secure in the knowledge that the oil is sterile, and when the cats wash their ears they will get a tiny but beneficial amount of vitamin E instead of the mineral oil, which washes vitamins E, A, and D out of the system.

Remember, anything you put onto the cat's body will eventually be licked off and swallowed. And oils will also be absorbed through the skin. So, if you're ever in doubt about using some substance on or around a cat, just ask yourself if you would mind if he or she lapped up a teaspoonful of it.

Step 9: The Catnip Party and Admiration

At the end of every grooming, even the daily sixty-second grooming, you must make every effort to convince your cats that in being groomed they have performed the cleverest of feats. Assure them that the grooming has revealed anew all their natural beauty, their wealth of symmetry and grace. Stroke their favorite spots to end the grooming on a high level of sensual pleasure.

You cannot give catnip every day, or the cats will lose their taste for it. But once every two weeks or once a month present catnip after the grooming. Alternate treats are brewer's yeast tablets, liver tablets, or any one of the treat foods you have on hand. Because this is between meals, the amount should be minuscule—less than a quarter teaspoonful in all. Follow up with a short play time to nicely cap off the grooming.

The Bath

Whenever anybody asks, "Can you give a cat a bath?" they always ask it in hushed tones, as if it were almost unthinkable. The bath is easy. Bathing a cat is really quite simple if you know how to go about it. A bath is luxurious and pleasant—warm, gentle, and sweet-smelling. Cats love to be clean, to be massaged, to be crooned over. A bath is all these things. A bath can be a wonderful demonstration of love, physical affection, and sensual pleasure.

Many cats never need a bath. If they're on the proper diet, they may never need one their whole life long. However, there are special circumstances where I would definitely recommend that the cat be bathed—at the end of a flea treatment, if the cat has soiled himself with diarrhea, if the cat gets into something, or if something is spilled on him.

It doesn't hurt a cat to be bathed any more than it hurts you to have your hair washed. But it's much better if the cat's general health is on such a plane of perfection that bathing becomes superfluous. A cat who needs to be bathed every month because he's greasy has a health problem. A cat with kidney failure will require frequent bathing; a cat with pancreas malfunction will also have a greasy coat. The bath doesn't solve the health problem—it just gets rid of the symptoms for a couple of days.

When new clients present me with a cat that has an oily coat and ask me to give a bath, I always inform them that it is against my policy to bathe any cat until he has been on the proper diet for one month. (I make an exception for a cat that has been soiled in any way.) I explain this rule thus: If I'm going to ask a cat to stand still for bathing and stand still for drying and comb out, I feel that that cat deserves to stay looking clean and terrific for at least a couple of months after the bath. If the cat's coat is greasy and full of dandruff because of a slow metabolism and low-quality diet full of waste products, the cat will still continue to exude old wastes through the pores in the form of oil and dandruff for at least another two or three weeks after beginning the high-quality diet. By then the backlog of wastes is gone. So I tell the owner to put the cat on the proper diet, remove food between meals, increase activity, and then in a month I'll come back and bathe the cat. Then, when I do come back, often the cat looks so great that I can say, "Are you sure you want Samantha bathed? I really don't think she needs it." I love to be able to say that, and the owners are always so proud. Young cats respond fast to the dietary change—some old cats do too. You never know until you try.

But if the cat's oily coat has resulted in the dust-mop effect, a bath may be just the thing he needs.

What do you need to give a bath? A cotton ball, some plain eye salve or Vaseline, three or four bath towels (you may not need them all), the cat's comb (no slicker brushes are used here), a hand-held hair dryer, a pure Castile shampoo for oily hair, and a hose that will connect to the faucet of either the kitchen sink or the bathtub. The hose should be the type used in barber shops and beauty parlors for rinsing hair. For pussy-cat bathing, you must cut off the spray end so the water comes out of the hose in a stream—a wide spray is just what you do *not* want.

In giving the bath, you are aiming for clean, virgin hair because virgin hair sheds dust and dirt. Do not use any shampoos with additives such as conditioners, lanolin, and so on. Most pet store shampoos have these additives. They are undesirable because they coat the hair follicle and give you the dust-mop effect again, which is just what you're trying to get rid of. I use Thionium, which I buy by the case from the veterinarian. Don't use a baby shampoo because it is too mild (you wash your hair once a week or more, but the cat gets a bath once or twice a year). If you can't find a pure Castile veterinary shampoo without undesirable additives, look for a pure Castile people shampoo—the strongest possible. Usually a formula for oily hair will be stronger. Try the cosmetic section in a health food store.

To prepare for the bath, first groom the cat to a fare-thee-well. Never wet the cat's coat while there are mats or even loose hair present. The very best plan is to groom the cat in the morning and bathe in the afternoon. That way you're not asking the cat to hold still for a long period at one time. Do a one-minute combing right before the bath.

Next set up the dryer, the comb, and three or four towels in a comfortable place away from the bath where you can sit with the cat on your lap and dry him. Adjust the dryer setting so that you have a good, strong stream of air but *not too much heat*. The temperature should be warm, never hot or cold. When it's properly set to your satisfaction, turn the dryer off.

Then mix a solution of half shampoo and half warm water into a dish or, better yet, an empty squeeze bottle. Shampoo must be warm and soothing, not cold and shocking. Attach the hose to the spigot and warm the tub or sink that you're going to use by swishing hot water around in it. The cat must be standing on pleasant warmth. Regulate the water temperature so that the stream of water coming through the hose is a tiny bit warmer than baby bath temperature. The cat's body temperature is normally higher than ours. Test the temperature against the inside of your forearm. If you love it, your cat will love it. Let the water continue to run from now until the end of the bath.

While you're letting the water run a bit, put about a quarter of a cotton ball into each of the cat's ears. You don't have to stuff it down, just make sure it is secure. The cotton will absorb any stray droplet that might spash that way. A drop of water in the ear wouldn't hurt, but there's a chance the cat might be startled, and because it's not sterile it could start an infection.

Then take the eye salve or Vaseline and apply a drop to the underside of the lower lid of each eye. This will provide a film of oiliness over the edge, protecting the eyes from any stray drops of water.

Don't begin to wet the cat until you're sure that the water temperature is going to remain constant throughout the bath. Put one towel within easy reach of the bath area to receive the cat afterward. In the wintertime, many finicky owners like to heat the towel on a radiator or in front of the oven.

Now the sink or tub is warm, the shampoo is warm, the water is warm, and the towel is warming. As you prepare each of these things, think of it as a gift you are going to give your cat. Consciously realize how much you would enjoy each of these facets of the bath.

Back in the first year that I was grooming, before I had developed my techniques, my biggest concern was that the cats should not be frightened. In my zeal to reassure them, I myself would lie in the tub with the cat on top of me, attempting to demonstrate that it must be perfectly safe, or I would surely be drowned first. Although this did work pretty well as far as calming the cat, I found it was rather difficult to give a thorough shampooing while lying supine with the cat standing on my stomach. Besides, I felt that it didn't give a very professional impression, because I had to be either nude or wearing a bathing suit.

Now, after eight years of experience and with my technique developed to a fine art, I still get wet. Oh, it's not that there is ever any wild splashing or thrashing about; the bath is still calm and luxurious. But there is just no substitute for the assurance that close physical proximity can give. You will want to nestle your cat close not only to your face but with your arms as well. I wear a sleeveless cotton smock that dries in a jiffy. Although I prefer to work in the kitchen sink, if I have to use the tub I wear shorts because I will be kneeling in the wet.

Now arrange the hose on the floor of the tub or sink so the water is calmly running down the drain. No splashes or gushes, please. Pick up the cat and say that you're going to make him feel good. Place him in the tub or sink. *If you're using the sink,* start by placing his hind paws in the sink and his front paws on the drainboard. Hold the cat close to you—do a lot of nuzzling with your face near his head and neck. Having your face close to his in a new and unfamiliar situation is very reassuring. *If you're using the tub,* it's best if you get into the tub carrying your cat. With your back to the spigot and drain, take the kneeling position as if to pill the cat (see Chapter 7) by backing the cat in toward you so that both you and the cat are facing the back of the tub. In both these cases, you are playing down the water aspect. The cat hasn't really seen or felt much water yet.

If the cat reacts as if trying to tell you, "Hey, watch out, there's water here—I'm liable to get wet," immediately put your face up next to his and reply that you know about the water. Tell him that it's going to feel good, it's warm, and it will make him nice and clean. You must explain everything you are doing, because the cat will be reading your tone, and your words will carry the desired emotional concept. Continuing to talk and nuzzle, pick up the hose so the end where the water comes out is nestled in your palm. The cat still hasn't seen it. Before you introduce the sight of the hose, introduce the pleasant, warm feeling of it by rubbing your hand containing the hose against his haunch. As you nuzzle him and describe in detail how much you love nice warm water, wet his thighs, lower back, sides, inner thighs, upper back, shoulders, and chest—in that order. Throughout all this, you must tenaciously hang on to the truth of the situation—the water feels fabulous. By this time, he will be standing in a quarter inch or so of water sloshing about in the bottom of the tub or sink. He may find this alarming and assume that you are not aware of this shocking development. Continuing the nuzzling, you must make two things crystal clear to him. First, you are fully aware of his concern and the reason for it and, second, you are doing what you are doing on purpose because it is marvelous and will make him feel wonderful if only he gives it a chance. Remember, if a cat is upset, he's upset because of fear of the *unknown,* not because of any kind of discomfort or *actual* danger. I call it suffering from an attack of the "what ifs." It's easy to understand—we humans do it all the time.

Now touch the hose to the floor in front of him and let him see the water running out. Still nuzzling, go back and redo his thighs, back, and so forth. This will prevent any chill. But this time continue on to include the throat and the back of the neck. Do not bathe the cat's face, forehead, or ears except when specifically soiled or when treating for fungus. Cats do pretty well in those areas by themselves. You can always wipe those areas off later with a damp cloth.

Now the cat's coat is thoroughly saturated with water. If the coat is greasy, you may have to go over it several times before it will hold the water. Before you apply the shampoo, lay the hose out of the way on the bottom of the sink or tub with the stream of water pointing down the drain so the cat feels he can safely forget about it. If you are working in the tub, you can hold the hose in place with one foot. Now you are going to focus the cat's attention on one of the biggest pleasures of the bath. Apply the fragrant shampoo solution to the neck, throat, shoulders, chest, armpits, upper back, lower back, tail, tummy, and inner thigh—in that order. If there's a problem area, such as lower back or tail greasiness or a soil or stain anywhere, apply the shampoo in that area first. Massage the cat's body, working up a nice foamy lather all over. This step really makes the cat feel fabulous. During this step, reapply warm water every thirty seconds so the cat doesn't feel chilled.

If you're working with a greasy coat and you fail to get a good lather on the first shampooing, don't worry about it. You always do two soapings anyway, so you can save the really fabulous massage for the second soaping when the shampoo is good and foamy. An owner never has a better opportunity than during the bath to explore the incredible musculature of the cat. Keep up a running commentary to your cat in which you exclaim about the quality of his muscles and the delicacy of each bone your fingers encounter. As your fingers explore the cat's symmetry and grace, express delight in audible exclamation of appreciation. In trusting you so far as to submit to such a very odd ritual, your cat is in effect giving you a tremendous gift—confidence and love.

To rinse be careful to hold the hose right at its tip. *Never let the cat see water flying at him.* Rinse in the same order that you applied the shampoo, starting high on the neck so that the dirty shampoo runs down and off the legs. Rinse it off the back, off the sides, and so on, leaving the legs, paws, and tail until last.

Be thorough with the rinse. Soap left in the coat is sticky and produces the dust-mop effect. It is also itchy and causes matting in Persians. You can get away with a little mistake in any other step, but this one must be perfect. Give special attention to rinsing the tail, skirts, outer thighs, inner thighs, and lower chest: in other words, all those places where matting tends to occur. During the rinsing, continue to nuzzle your face close to the cat's face as much as possible and call attention to the way the water is making him nice and warm again and how the nasty oiliness and dirt are being washed away down the drain.

When the coat is squeaky clean and free of soap, get rid of some of the water by pressing the coat against the skin and very lightly squeezing his legs, paws, and tail. Grab the warm towel from the radiator or stove and bundle the cat up in it, telling him that this warm towel and the forthcoming warm dryer is the reward for the heroic patience he has displayed. Carry him out to the drying area. Drape another towel across your lap and fold him in another dry towel (the first towel is probably wet by now). The more towels you use, the faster he'll get dry.

To introduce the dryer, use the same principle you used when introducing the water. Break the dryer up into its component parts—sound, sensation, and sight. As you're toweling the neck, nuzzling the cat's cheek, and telling him how delicious he smells, hold the dryer far away with your other hand well out of his sight. Continue talking to him and casually turn the dryer on, ignoring it completely and continuing to focus on the delicious-smelling cat.

Proceeding on to the feel of the dryer (making sure he cannot see it yet), slowly introduce the stream of comfortably warm air against the thigh or lower back. Try to always have your hand or finger on his body *included* in the path of that warm stream of air, so that you can judge the temperature. *The dryer must always be kept slowly moving.* If you hold it still, it will burn. Remember that the cat's skin is extremely delicate and sensitive. Think of the mucuous membrane lining the inside of your lower lip. If you treat all the cat's body as if it were that sensitive, you'll always keep him safe.

The cat will probably move and want to get up. Turn the dryer off when this happens, readjust his position, and perhaps take a fresh towel. Drying is much more difficult to do alone. It goes three times faster if you can find someone to hold the cat on a lap and distract him while you apply the dryer in one hand and the towel in the other. Allow the cat to see the dryer at a time when it has already been turned on and directed against the body for a couple of seconds. (Remember to keep the dryer moving.)

After the hair is more than half dry all over, begin combing with a wide-toothed comb as you dry. An assistant is invaluable here, because combing and blow-drying simultaneously speeds the drying about 300 percent. If you're alone, you have to go from one to the other. The comb is in the right hand, and the dryer is in the left hand. Comb ever so lightly, and again be sure to keep the dryer moving. Combing separates the hair so the stream of air can dry it even faster.

When drying the neck or throat, cup one hand over the cat's ears, eyes, and nose so that the stream of air from the dryer is never directed there. The cat can take care of drying those areas himself with his paw and tongue. It's also very easy for him to dry feet and ankles. Although the tail is easy enough for him to reach, the hair there is usually longer and thicker, so it's good to give him a good headstart by using the dryer on the tail.

You don't have to get him absolutely dry, especially during the summer or in a well-heated apartment. However, the cat must be dry enough so you can easily run the comb through the hair all over the body. Otherwise long-haired cats may mat. Even if you try your best to get a cat completely dry, it's almost impossible. Anyway, cats reach their peak of fluffy beauty the day after a bath. When you decide to call it quits and put the cat down, go all out with positive reinforcement. If you have a brass band available, strike it up now. Tell your cat that he or she is not only the bravest and the most patient but also the softest and the most gloriously beautiful creature with the most delectable scent on God's green earth. Repeat your rhapsodic performance at intervals all during the rest of the day. It won't be difficult to do. You'll understand what I mean the first time you experience a freshly bathed cat. Chances are you won't be able to keep your hands off those lovely furs. After the first bath, I always remind owners that after the cat has been on the high-quality diet for a while this is the way he or she will always look and feel.

Two or three times a year, I run into cats who are afraid of the dryer.

If you follow all the prescribed steps in introducing the dryer and yet the cat has a reaction verging on hysteria when you turn it on, don't persist. Just turn up the heat in the room, turn on the oven, and towel dry like crazy, using about eight or nine towels. Keep at it until you can successfully run the comb through all the hair. Your cat will still look beautiful tomorrow, just like a cat that has been blown dry.

If you are bathing cats because they have fleas, refer to the section entitled "Does My Cat Have Fleas?" in Chapter 7. Hopefully your cat does not have fleas. If not, you have the option of applying the "ounce of prevention" principle. If you think there is the slightest chance of a single flea rearing its ugly head anywhere near your cat, you may want to add the herbal flea repellant, oil of pennyroyal, to the second soaping, as described in Chapter 7.

One word about dry shampoo—forget it. It coats the hair, and it just doesn't work well. The tiny bit of oil it absorbs could be done away with much more efficiently by using simple cornstarch. So don't waste your money, and don't put harmful perfumes and chemicals on your cat's coat.

Grooming for Seasonal and Stress Situations

Most of my new clients come to me either in the middle of the summer, after the big spring shed, or else they are people who have been away, come back, and found their Persian full of mats. The format is almost always the same. The hysterical owners call me and tell me they returned after a few weeks away to find the cat totally matted: "It's never happened before, and the cat won't let me comb him—can you help?" I always reassure the owners that I can put the cat back in shape again. But I ask them not to touch the mats until I get there. "Pretend to the cat that you've forgotten about the mats," I say. I don't want the cat to have a fresh memory of being hurt by someone fooling around with the mats.

Almost always the cats are grateful that I'm working on them once they catch on to what I'm doing. It happens again and again, and yet I'm always awed by how much a cat can understand. I get the owner to talk to the cat about interesting things that happen in the cat's life, and this helps the cat to focus on the beloved owner's voice rather than on the nerve-wracking process of Anitra cutting out the mats. The poor owners are always contrite, assuring me over and over again that this could not possibly have happened if they'd been home and it had certainly never happened before.

It doesn't ever have to happen again even if you do go away or some other stress situation occurs such as moving, sickness in the family, or anything that might be stressful to the cat and might keep you from the necessary daily grooming. All you have to do to prevent it is to plan in advance and take "a stitch in time." Half the battle is keeping the nutrition at a high level and doubling the amount of lecithin in the Vita-Mineral Mix during times of stress. This makes the hair easier to groom. If you know already that your cat has a tendency to either diarrhea or constipation when under stress, double the bran as well. If it is a Persian, trim more widely around the anus and inner thigh.

Be very specific about feeding instructions to whoever is going to take care of the cat. Now is certainly not the time to be lax. I am always surprised when owners do not give detailed instructions for feeding to the person taking care of the cat in their absence. Often they seem to feel that it's enough of an imposition to ask someone to care for the animal even if they're paying the person, and they don't want to inconvenience the sitter even more by asking for any sort of special dietary requirements. I tell these people that they are dead wrong.

First of all, sitters in general are very nice. Just put yourself in the place of the sitter. What most nice sitters want more than anything else is to be given as much information as possible about how best to keep your pet in top physical shape until you get back. Taking care of someone else's cat is a heavy responsibility, even if it is also a great delight.

Even if your sitter declares that he or she will enjoy combing the cat, it's safest to clip the hair short, at least in the armpits, around the anus, and along the inner thigh. How far you extend the clipping depends on whether your cat's coat is easy to groom or long, thick, and difficult to groom. The principle is to clip away any and all hair that might present a problem to the neophyte groomer. Remember when you began grooming the cat, and recall which areas of the cat's fur tend to mat up first. You will definitely want to clip those areas shorter than an inch.

Clarence Eckroate's coat is sparse and silky. It's supereasy to groom, and Clarence's personality falls under the heading of "old sweetie pie." Normally we don't even clip his armpits. However, if Norma were to take a business trip in the middle of the shedding season, I would advise a modest trim in the armpits and around the anus just to be on the safe side.

Pandy Kauffman's coat is quite thick. Besides, she is a high-strung cat who has never learned to enjoy her groomings. Her owner, Diane, and I have decided that it's wise to keep a jump ahead of the mats by clipping Pandy's armpits, leg crease, anus, and inner thigh every single month. Pandy is nervous enough during her normal monthly grooming, which she barely puts up with. If a mat forms anywhere in the furs, Pandy knows it, focuses on it, and imagines all kinds of dire consequences that could befall her during that mat's removal. With Pandy, it's much wiser and kinder to clip too much rather than too little.

When Diane Kauffman, Pandy's owner, goes away, we go all out—stopping just short of the "Cape Cod Clip" (discussed later). We trim down to less than a quarter inch all the hair on Pandy's abdomen, inner thighs, armpits, and chest. I extend the clipping line of the armpits and leg creases right up Pandy's sides toward the shoulder blades and hip bones respectively. When we're finished and place Pandy on the floor, she gives an irate shake, and as she stalks off one can see that she has so much fluffiness left that no one would ever be able to detect our sneaky clipping without turning Pandy upside down. Knowing Pandy, I can't see how that's likely to happen.

Sammy Levy's coat is the longest and thickest that I've ever seen. Sammy is a fabulous brown tabby Persian. His ruff hairs measure about four and half inches from root to tip. Sammy is a darling, but his health is rather delicate, and there have been a couple of times over the years when Sammy's coat became greasy and full of dandruff as a result of a breakdown in his physical health. He enjoys grooming to a certain extent but is supersensitive, and when he falls ill that sensitivity increases.

During his first illness, his owner and I agreed that Sammy's comfort came first. We sacrificed the beautiful, thick, soft hair of his inner thighs, abdomen, chest, etc. I gave him the same sort of clip I used on Pandy. With Sammy, I also took off part of the skirts and the fronts of the thighs. The clipping was so extensive that one could easily see the difference in Sammy's shape as he walked about. But Sammy loved it. On hot summer days, he'd lay his abdomen against the cool bathroom tiles and sleep with a contented smile on his face. Because the worst areas of potential matting were now eliminated, Sammy could again relax and enjoy the luxury of his biweekly grooming during his convalescence.

One thing I do every month when I see my regular clients is clip off all the fur in the armpits and about a half-inch of fur around the anus in a circle because these are the prime areas for matting. If the bloomers are full and fluffy, I also clip a "free-fall area" underneath the anus by removing some of the hair from the bloomers on the back of the inner thighs.

When I clip armpits and the anal area, I cut the hair down to less than a sixteenth of an inch. No one but you and the pussycat will know that beneath that fluffy exterior the armpits are bare—unless, of course, your cat does a lot of waving.

To satisfy public demand, I have had to devise what I dub "the Cape Cod Clip." This is for owners who are taking their cats on summer vacation to woodsy, weedy, sandy, buggy areas full of briars and brambles. I had to think of a way to protect the cat from the sun from above, leave most of the ruff and tail, to satisfy the cat psychologically; and get rid of most of the cat's hair because the owners didn't want to bother with it under the wilderness circumstances. At the same time, my professional eye insisted that I end up with a cat who was still esthetically pleasing.

I dubbed it "the Cape Cod Clip" in honor of the first cat I tried it on. She was, as you may have guessed, bound for Cape Cod. She was an elderly tabby Persian with a medium-thick coat. I did the extensive clipping in the armpits, extending the clipping all the way up on both sides of the chest and then clipped the chest fur down to a half inch. Beginning with the lower part of the ruff, I left the hair longer and longer to blend the short chest hair in with her medium-length ruff. When working on a cat with a very long ruff of three or four inches, I usually trim the ruff hair down so it is no longer than two inches. I trim the leg creases, inner thighs, abdomen, and backs of thighs down to an eighth of an inch or less. If the cat has long, silky ankle feathers, I trim them right down, leaving the leg fur about a quarter inch long. I trim the outer thighs down to a quarter or half inch, and about halfway up the thigh I allow the length of hair to increase so that, for about three inches on both sides of the spine, the hair is left at normal length to protect the cat from the sun. That area is very easy to groom, anyway.

From the long hair around the top of the cat's back to the very short hair on the abdomen, I simply taper gradually. For esthetic reasons, you may want to cut off as much as a half inch from the tail but *only near the anus* in order to taper the tail into the anal clip. Caution: Don't cut the hair on the tail unless it's matted or badly soiled. Tail hair takes many months to grow in again.

On returning from Cape Cod, the tabby Persian's owner informed me that she was frequently asked what kind of a cat she had. People thought her cat was quite lovely and wondered where they could get one like her. She had a hard time convincing them that Mimi was a classic tabby Persian wearing her Cape Cod Clip.

Stud Tail

It seems appropriate here to mention stud tail. Although I consider stud tail a health problem, most people consider it a grooming problem, so I include it in this chapter. Stud tail is a disease of the sebaceous glands found along the top of the tail and up the base of the spine. It happens when these glands oversecrete sebaceous fluid and the pores become clogged. The excess fluid becomes hardened into a substance closely resembling half-dried ear wax. It is waxy rather than oily and usually dark brown or black.

Stud tail, as the name implies, is found on almost all unneutered males but unfortunately is not limited to them. I've seen it on females, too, when food is left available between meals and the diet is not up to par.

I have noticed that every year at the cat show someone comes up with what he or she claims is a sure-fire cure for stud tail. These cures always involve spraying, powdering, or dipping the tail into something. The reason why there is always a new cure every year is that none of them work. Many breeders who show cats have their own private "secrets" that they hold to despite their inefficiency and the possible health hazards involved in implementing some of the more bizarre "solutions." I have been made privy to such secrets as the use of dishwashing detergent, kerosene, and Windex. Forget it. Stud tail is a result of what is happening inside the cat's body due to a backup of wastes. It is caused by poor feeding and a slowdown of the metabolism. You can't cure stud tail from the outside.

However, I too have a secret remedy, temporary though it may be. This is the best method I have found to date and is to be used in the beginning, while the new, improved diet is slowly doing its work to permanently eradicate the disease. That hard, waxy grease cannot be washed off by any kind of detergent, soap, alcohol, or you-name-it. It's impossible. So don't wash it off. Instead, heavily powder the area with plain cornstarch, which will absorb the greasy exudation. Then comb, shake, and jiggle the greasy cornstarch out. Do it again a couple more times and then wash with the usual shampoo. This cornstarch trick can also be used around the ears after an oily ear medication. Cornstarch is harmless—it has no perfumes or conditioners. Nothing I have found is more efficient. Here's another case where the cheapest and easiest also turns out to be the best.

A cat with stud tail will be supersensitive. The pores and glands are usually inflamed and sore, so be extremely gentle. Don't worry—if the cat is neutered, and on the correct diet and no longer smells food between meals, the condition will gradually disappear.

Home Care of Sick Cats

Any concerned owner follows the veterinarian's advice word for word if his or her pussycat is ill. But most people wish they could do even more to help bring their cat back to rosy health. Well, you can do more. You can be aware of the little extras that can make the difference so your cat recovers speedily and stays at optimum health thereafter.

Stress: A Cat's Natural Enemy

For a good many years now, the role played by stress in diseases of the human body has been a major concern. In cats, the link between stress and illness is even stronger. Cats have a lower threshold of stress than humans have. This means that things not ordinarily stressful to us sometimes can actually be painful to a cat. The cat's sense of smell, for example, is so highly developed as to make ours seem virtually nonexistent by comparison.

Beside the cat's supersensitivity to physical stresses such as sharp smells, loud noise, or extremes in temperature, the cat is also extremely sensitive to emotional stress. The loss of a loved one, be it animal or human, often sends the cat's emotions plunging into depression and even beyond, into deep mourning. Such hopeless sadness, if left unchecked, drains the system and leaves the body open to invasion by any germ or virus that happens along.

In the normal course of life, cats can usually handle stress pretty well. But when the cat is faced with multiple stresses, extreme stresses, or prolonged stress, the body's reserves of energy are drained to a danger point. Cats faced with too much stress over too long a period of time become tense and nervous and then begin to withdraw. I've noticed that families who habitually hold two or three conversations simultaneously and therefore always speak in a shout also have shy, nervous cats who can usually be found huddled away in the darkest corner of a back bedroom closet. Cats cannot feel at ease in a stress-filled environment. It is obvious to them that they are not safe, and they live in a constant state of readiness for the next assault on their senses.

Cats in such situations are faced with prolonged stress that wears on their nerves and eventually leaves them vulnerable to disease. A germ, virus, or fungus that the cats would normally throw off can take hold easily if all their resistance has been depleted dealing with stress.

Stress can also be a trigger that activates any latent disease or lurking pathological condition within the body. When the same disease or condition is repeatedly activated by any stressful situation in a cat's life, it is referred to as that cat's "stress target." When confronted with a feline client who tends to get any particular disease again and again, I always question the owner about what was happening in the household immediately preceding the onset of the disease. Was the family away on a trip and the cat left alone? Did the family have visitors—perhaps young and active visitors? Or perhaps the painters came—moving furniture out of place and causing an excruciating smell?

It's a generally accepted fact that cystitis, although caused by a combination of germs and the presence of ash in the diet, is emotionally triggered. However, almost any illness, from upper respiratory infection to foot fungus, can become active if too much stress in the environment lowers resistance to the point where a cat's particular weakness can take hold and thrive.

Granted, there will be many times in the life of the cat and its human family when you must knowingly subject your cat to serious stress. So, to avoid having your cat succumb to an illness, simply recognize stress situations for what they are and then make an extra effort to eliminate or at least cushion all other stresses in the environment that you can control.

Our problem is to determine what exactly constitutes stress to a cat, as opposed to a human, a dog, or other small animal. Here's a list of some stresses a cat may encounter, along with suggestions as to how to cope with them. In a majority of cases, common sense goes a long way.

- *Any surprise.* Announce your intentions before doing anything—touching the cat, turning on the light, and so on.

- *Loud noise.* Caution all visitors to speak in calm and soothing tones. If there is unavoidable noise in another part of the home, put a portable radio near the cat's resting place and tune it to soothing classical music.

- *Owner being upset or unhappy.* If you have serious problems, put them up on a mental shelf while spending time with a cat. Bring into your conscious mind positive thoughts of love and constructive plans about how you can make your cat more comfortable and hasten the sick cat's journey back to health.

- *Change in the cat's environment.* Confine the cat to a small area such as the bathroom where no change is taking place. Or surround your cat with as many familiar things (toys, favorite pillow, and so on) as possible.

- *Change to new environment.* Move the cat into one room that is already furnished with old, familiar furniture. Have the cat's litter box, food and water dishes, toys, and so on already there.

- *Introduction of visitors.* Any new person should be seated and should first give eye and voice contact before touching the cat. Then he or she should extend one hand only, palm down, below the cat's nose level. Allow the cat to sniff before the visitor touches the cat.

- *Absence of familiar people or being left alone.* See Chapter 9, the section entitled "While You're Away."

- *Being held down or restrained (during medical procedures such as an EKG).* Keep calm and loving thoughts in your mind. Announce your intentions. Try to feel that what you're doing is an extension of petting.

- *Confinement or caging.* Provide a brown paper bag in which the cat can hide, as described in Chapter 8, "Going to the Vet."

- *X-Rays, anesthetics, and medications.* First give the cat 500 units of vitamin C, as described later in this chapter in the section entitled "Nutritional Supports for Medication."

- *Surgery, catheterization, and wounds.* Give the cat vitamins C and E and cod liver oil, as described later in this chapter in the section entitled "Nutritional Supports for Medication."

- *Lack of a hiding place.* Give the cat a cardboard box or an opened brown paper bag.
- *Extremes of heat or cold.* Use a hot water bottle or an ice pack as described in Chapter 8, "Going to the Vet."
- *Sharp smells (tobacco smoke or chemicals).* Try to be aware, and you'll improve your own sense of smell and avoid stress for yourself, too.
- *Ash and additives in foods.* Read labels and avoid ash and additives.
- *Obesity.* See section on "Obesity" in this chapter.
- *Being soiled by excrement, medication, and so on.* Wipe it off at once before it hardens on the cat's fur.
- *Any infection or infestation.* Follow the veterinarian's orders.
- *Tooth tartar or cavities.* Dentistry should be done by the veterinarian as soon as the cat is well enough.
- *Pain.* Add one-half teaspoonful dolomite and one dropperful of cod liver oil to the cat's food. Dolomite is high in calcium, which has been proven effective as a relaxant and pain reliever. The cod liver oil is high in vitamin D, which the body needs to assimilate calcium.
- *Overfilling the stomach.* It's better to feed too little than too much. See the section entitled "Fasting and Force Feeding" in this chapter.
- *Food too hot or cold.* When in doubt, feel the cat's food with your finger.
- *Being unneutered.* Have the cat neutered by a competent veterinarian. See Chapter 5, "Neuter and Spay, It's the Kindest Way."

When caring for a cat who is already ill with a disease—in itself a major stress—minimize as many other stresses as possible in order to save the cat's energy, calories, adrenalin, and vital life force, so that they can be used to fight the disease. It is a gratifying experience for the sensitive owner to be able to raise the odds in a pet's favor in this way, especially when the pet is ill.

A Word About Administering Medications

When doing anything to cats—pilling, force feeding, grooming, and so on—it's best to try to indicate to them *beforehand* what you are trying to do. Don't have any secrets. Because fear of the unknown is the cat's greatest fear, if you can let him know what you want to do, even though he may not like it or may indicate an objection or try to leave, at least he will not become hysterical. If you keep him from leaving and controlling his objections as you proceed to gently have your way, chances are the whole thing will be over very quickly. He'll come to regard the experience as one of those bizarre acts that owners indulge in from time to time that are, on the one hand, mildly unpleasant and not to be understood, but, on the other hand, neither painful nor threatening. Because there's nothing a cat can do, he puts up with such acts out of the love he bears in his heart for you. After all, you have not been raised as a cat and therefore cannot be expected to be perfect in every way.

I find I can get away with an awful lot and save a great deal of wear and tear on the cat's nerves by making the cat believe that I am "petting" him. If I have to do any touching with the hands—it doesn't matter what the reason really is—if I truly believe in my heart that I am expressing love by doing this thing, then I can convey that feeling to the cat.

Cats do understand that humans are different from cats and have different ways of showing affection. For example, Marshmallow Goodfellow, an abandoned white short-hair, had to take six pills a day during treatment for cystitis brought on by bladder stones. Poor Marshmallow had spent his first four years before landing at my place consuming huge quantities of dry food and tuna fish. He was an enormous and fearsome-looking white male whose personality was best described by his name: Marshmallow. His craving for physical affection was so great that he would lift a paw and pat my trousers again and again to get attention and then throw himself on the floor at my feet, roll onto his back, and lick my ankle. When finally picked up and hugged, he liked to wrap his front legs around my neck and hug back, capping the joyful moment by vigorously washing my cheek.

I was very busy during his first weeks with me and never seemed to have enough time to fill completely Marshie's need for affection. Because cystitis is well known to be a stress-linked disease, I didn't want him to feel threatened because every time he saw me I started shoving a pill down his throat. I had to condition Marshmallow to believe that petting was petting no matter where he was touched and to set up a positive association between pilling and petting and love so that he would look forward to the pill rather than fearing it. It wasn't hard. All I did was to assume the kneeling pill-giving position (described later in this chapter) every time I petted him. Then I began to broaden his petting horizons, as it were, by stroking his legs, feet, thighs, and so on, along with all the usual places. I even included his lips and teeth. He gave me a doubtful look the first time but seemed to accept it philosophically thereafter. When I worked in the actual pilling procedure, that sweet animal accepted it along with all the rest. He looked forward to pilling time with happy anticipation as his own special petting time. And to this day that sweet animal still cherishes the belief that crazy Anitra likes to express affection by petting a pussycat's tongue.

Cats easily pick up your intentions, feelings, and emotions. So when you're going through all the steps leading up to pilling or wrapping the cat in a towel, or grooming, or whatever, think of each and every step along the way as separate from all the other steps, and fix it clearly in your own mind, that you are expressing love by doing it. In almost every case, you will be able to find a way to make each separate step feel good to the cat.

But first, before you begin, always remember to wash your hands. And, even more important, rinse them. Remember, the cat's sense of smell is many, many times sharper than yours. If someone wanted to pop a small piece of your favorite candy in your mouth, how would you accept it if, just as the hand approached your face, you caught a whiff of chemical or the odor of some bodily excretion. Good grief! Make sure your hand smells only like a hand.

Wrapping the Cat for Medication

As close as my cat Priscilla and I are, I always have to wrap her to give her medication. Otherwise she reaches up her left paw—Priscilla is left-handed—and keeps pushing my hand away so I'm not able to get the pill beyond the hump in her tongue and down her throat. I know she really wants to cooperate, and she wishes she could, but she simply can't control herself. Cats are like that. Sometimes, even though they want to cooperate, they need your help.

Wrapping the cat in a towel gives you much more control. Instead of the cat being almost an equal partner in the project, it puts you totally in command. The towel should not be thick, fluffy, nor expensive. The easiest towel to work with for wrapping is a smallish bath towel—thin and old.

Here is a suggested breakdown of the steps, but you can break any one of these steps down even further if you like.

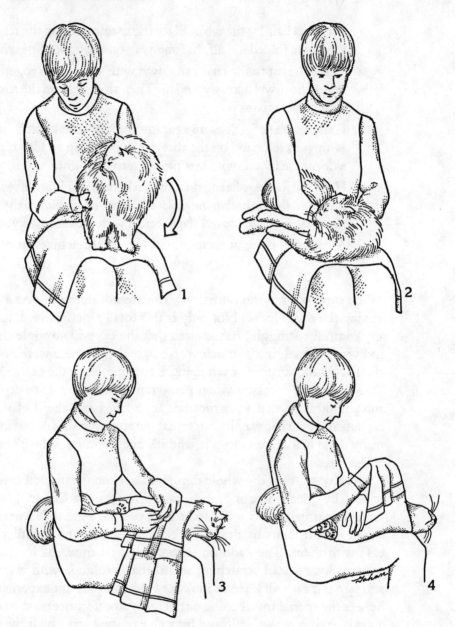

Figure 12
Wrapping the cat

1. Set up a chair by the table, place the medication on the table; put the towel folded in half the long way on the back of the chair.
2. Carry the cat to the chair; sit down with your knees together, and drape the towel across your lap. Then sit the cat on the towel facing away from you.
3. Grasp the cat's forelegs up near the chest in your right hand and, with your left hand on the rump, lift the cat up and lay him on his side on the towel, with feet pointing to the right.
4. Hold the forelegs flat against the cat's chest, fold the left towel flap, then fold the right flap *snugly* over the cat to pin down the forelegs securely. Hold the towel flaps secure with the inside of your knee.
5. Medicate the cat; unwrap him or her, and then give a treat.

Be sure to wrap the cat firmly. You are not doing the cat a favor by leaving the towel loose. Not only is this totally ineffective; but if there's any room for struggle, rest assured that the cat will struggle and thrash and work himself into a much worse state than if there were no towel at all. The whole purpose of wrapping is to immobilize the cat.

It's almost a necessity when you wrap a cat to be able to do it swiftly and smoothly so that your motions are a few beats ahead of what your cat anticipates. That way he can't imagine anything dire or terrible; it's already done before he knows it, and it's not terrible at all—it's only snug and secure.

As always, turn the whole thing into a demonstration of love accompanied by much nuzzling and praise. You might like to practice the wrapping ritual once a week to be sure you have the skill whenever you might need it. Start by practicing only Steps 1, 2, and 3 until you are at ease with them. Then add one more step at a time. As long as you're doing a lot of head scratching and throat stroking, with a treat afterwards, your cat will learn to look forward to a pleasant experience when he sees the special towel come out. This is a perfect occasion to end with a yeast or liver tablet, followed by a nice mutual scratch on the post or a chase after the toughie mouse.

Here again that same old number one rule applies: *patience*. Because during practice runs you are not under any pressure to actually get medication into the cat, you can begin by spending the first two or three sessions just stroking him around the armpits and shoulders, which you will later be grasping to lift and turn him over. That way you'll learn how the leg bones feel, where the underarm tendons are, and so on.

I feel sorry for owners who never get beyond stroking their pet's back and head. Cats are very sensual, and finicky owners want to know their pet's whole body—bloomers and inner thigh, foreleg muscles and shins, paw and claw. Explore the bone structure and musculature as if you were giving a massage—your cat will love it.

Nutritional Supports for Medications

All medications have some undesirable side effects. These side effects can range anywhere from destroying the cells of the liver or kidney to depleting or washing out one or more vitamins or minerals from the body. I reason that if a cat needs some medication because he is sick, then he must have it. But, once we know what the side effects are, we need not accept them as inevitable. As long as we know *what* they are, we can attempt to control or at least mitigate these negative factors.

When a cat of mine is given a pill, I always want to know what it is—what family or category it fits into—antibiotics, diuretics, cortisone and other steroids, anesthetics and tranquilizers, or mineral oil. I then tell the doctor what I intend to do in terms of adjusting the diet and adding nutrients or vitamin supplements. I want to be sure that any changes I make do not in any way aggravate the cat's special problem or interfere with the action of the medication.

There are five categories of medication with which you will most frequently have to deal, described in the following sections.

Antibiotics

Antibiotics are used to kill germs and sometimes viruses. If an antibiotic is taken orally in pill or liquid form, it will kill all the germs in the entire alimentary canal, from the mouth right on down to the anus, before it even begins to work on the germs it was sent after in the liver or the kidney or wherever the disease happens to be. Diarrhea is one way that the body reacts to the absence of all microorganisms in the intestinal tract. Not all bacteria are bad—a healthy body has lots of friendly bacteria in the intestines that manufacture some of the B vitamins, help with the absorption of nutrients, and help regulate the acid-alkaline balance in the intestine. When the antibiotic comes through the alimentary canal, these good bacteria bite the dust with all the rest. The absence of the good bacteria disrupts the acid-alkaline balance, and this causes diarrhea. You can replace the friendly bacteria that were destroyed by feeding about 3 cubic centimeters (cc) of acidophilus bacteria culture in water one hour after each administration of the antibiotic. The companies Plus Products and Continental both market an acidophilus culture suspended in water, not milk. Milk and milk products such as yogurt do not mix well with antibiotics. Also, many adult cats can't digest milk, even when they're healthy. Because that bottled acidophilus won't keep more than two weeks in the refrigerator, I like to mix a quarter teaspoonful of it into all the cat's dinners when I have it in the house.

Continue mixing the acidophilus culture into the food for two weeks after the course of the antibiotic is finished. It's very good for the insides of the intestines. Some antibiotics, such as Keflex, are so harsh and strong that the poor little pussycat will still get diarrhea even though he's getting the acidophilus chaser after each medication. Keep it up anyway, he'd be a lot worse off without it. It will help him bounce back faster once the nasty medicine is finished.

Remember that when the veterinarian gives you antibiotics you must be sure to follow the directions very carefully. Unlike diuretics and cortisone, antibiotics are not given for the shortest time possible. You must give the full course of antibiotics that the doctor prescribes, finishing all the pills. If you're careless and stop too soon, a stray germ or two might survive, slightly injured, to breed an altogether new strain of germ, which is then immune to that antibiotic and a brand-new menace to all the pussycats of the world.

Diuretics

Diuretics are given to prevent water retention. They help the body drain liquid by promoting copious urination. If there is fluid present—in the lungs, abdomen, or around the heart—a diuretic may be prescribed. Lasix is one type of diuretic. Usually the cat will begin to drink copiously and urinate copiously. And, hopefully, the bad fluid will be drawn to the kidneys and bladder and make its exit with the good fluid. However, with all this washing of fluids through the body, many water-soluble nutrients, vitamins, and minerals will be washed out along with everything else. The biggest loss is potassium. If a cat is given a diuretic, get some

Adolf's Salt Substitute and sprinkle a sixteenth of a teaspoonful or so onto the cat's food at each meal. Double the amount of Vita-Mineral Mix with each meal to provide more of the other trace minerals and water-soluble vitamins that may be washed away. Diuretics are almost never given over long periods of time.

Cortisone and Other Steroids

Steroids are sometimes used to reduce inflammation and swelling. However, steroids raise the body's need for vitamins A and C. If a cat is put on steroids or cortisone, give 250 units of vitamin C a day and a dropperful of cod liver oil every other day. Because steroids are usually given to reduce swelling, you probably are already giving your cat extra vitamin C and cod liver oil to alleviate the condition.

One caution about steroids: Never stop them abruptly. Steroids, like diuretics, are always given for as short a time as possible, and the dose is always tapered down at the end. Steroids can make cats feel depressed. Coming off the steroids too abruptly depresses them even more.

Anesthetics, Tranquilizers, and X-Rays

Vitamin C is manufactured by cats in their intestines. This takes care of the normal requirements. However, "normal" means hunting twice a day and lounging in the sun—healthy, happy cats. It has been found that any stress can cause vitamin C to be totally depleted—extreme cold, extreme heat, fear, anger, after X-rays, during any illness, or after anesthetic. Even a disruption in the owner's life can be stressful to the sensitive cat. The vitamin C requirement during such situations soars. It is practically impossible to get an overdose of vitamin C, because it cannot be stored. Excess vitamin C is excreted in the urine. That's why it is sometimes used as a way to acidify the urine in cases of cystitis. I give 250 units of vitamin C twice a day for two days before a cat is to be either X-rayed or anesthetized. I give it again for three days afterward, in hopes of keeping the cat's resistance to disease higher. Anesthetization is such a drain on the cat's body that all too often the cat picks up some unrelated infection that becomes evident a couple of days after the return home. See Chapter 8, "Going to the Vet."

I think of vitamin C as a little additional cushion to help the beleaguered body cope with any serious stress. At the risk of belaboring a point, let me say again that the entire nutritional program must be of extra high quality during stress. Anesthetic is one of the worst stresses. Vitamin C is a big help, but vitamin C can't do it alone. You need the vitamin B family and vitamin E to complete the antistress group.

Mineral Oil

Mineral oil washes the oil-soluble vitamins A, D, and E out of the system. Fur ball medications and laxatives such as Petromalt and Laxitone contain mineral oils. If the doctor advises their use, follow them with a seven-day regimen of replacing those fat-soluble vitamins. Give the cat one-half teaspoonful (one dropperful) of cod liver oil and a drop of vitamin E squeezed out of a 100-unit capsule every day for seven days after giving mineral oil in any form.

Surgery and Catheterization

I'll add a word here about nutritional support before and after surgery and catheterization. These procedures present the body with two problems: stress and scarring. This means that nutrition should emphasize the antistress vitamins as described in the section for Anesthetics and X-rays. In addition, to reduce the amount of scar tissue needed, add a plentiful supply of vitamin E to the diet. I give 100 units of vitamin E for two days before and two days after surgery and then one drop every day until the stitches come out and the scar is healed. To prevent the healing scar from itching, you can rub vitamin E directly on the scar once the scab is gone.

Dandruff

Dandruff is a waste product. As discussed in Chapter 2, when the smell of food triggers the brain to prepare the body for digestion, waste disposal is slowed down tremendously, along with the rest of the metabolism. So, if the owner leaves food available between meals, the cat constantly smells food and the metabolism is constantly slow. The result is that wastes build up and back up. Disposing of those wastes and toxins is just as important as taking in food. When the primary avenues of excretion—the kidneys and the intestines—are not able to handle all these wastes, the wastes get rerouted through the secondary routes: through the lungs, as carbon dioxide, and the pores of the skin, as grease and dandruff. Ninety percent of all cats with dandruff have owners who allow their cats to smell food all day long by leaving some sort of food or a dirty food bowl on the floor between meals and/or by giving frequent snacks or treats. Dry food is the usual culprit here. Dandruff almost always disappears when no food smell lingers between meals and when lecithin granules are added to the diet to help emulsify the fatty wastes so the blood and urine can carry them away and send them out through the usual channels.

Weight Loss

In the finicky eater syndrome, if the smell of food triggers the brain and if the cat is smelling food every time he passes the food dish or a vagrant breeze wafts the odor his way, sooner or later that trigger mechanism wears out and the cat begins to eat less. Ninety percent of all finicky eaters have owners who leave food available between meals or give frequent snacks. Often finicky eaters also have dandruff. Add to this a slowed metabolism, which results in inefficient digestion, and you have a skinny, undernourished cat surrounded by food. Because circulation and respiration are slower, less blood and oxygen are reaching the organs. Less blood pumping through the organs means the cat will age earlier. A cat who smells food all day long cannot live as long as he could have if his owner cleared away all food between meals.

If a cat is not eating because he is very old or recovering from illness (some antibiotics tend to suppress appetite) a very good way to tempt him is with Chicken Yeast Soup. It is made in the following way:

High-Calcium Broth (Chicken Yeast Soup)

Save up bones from one or two chickens in your freezer. Crack and break up the bones if you can, exposing the marrow. Simmer two to three hours in a large pot of water to which the juice of one-quarter· lemon has been added (acid dissolves the calcium out of the bones). Don't let the water boil away, but do let it boil down to a concentrated amount just covering the bones. Strain the broth and store it in the refrigerator for use in cat food or as Chicken Yeast Soup by bringing the broth to room temperature and adding one teaspoonful of yeast per half-cup broth.

I used to bring Chicken Yeast Soup with me when I was working night duty at Dr. Rowan's Cat Practice. Very often cats who could not be tempted even with baby food would break their fast for Chicken Yeast Soup. The liquid will keep a sick cat from dehydrating. Also, it is high in protein, calcium, phosphorus, and the B vitamins.

When trying for weight gain in elderly cats or cats depleted from sickness, give three or four moderate-sized meals a day. Don't feed large meals, because they are too hard to digest and assimilation will not proceed efficiently. Always leave at least four hours between meals, for the same reasons.

Obesity

Obesity is another problem that can be caused by leaving food available between meals. If cats are on a low-quality diet, their bodies will be reaching for the nutrients that are missing in the food. The cats will eat too much of the available food in an effort to supply those nutrients. The low-quality diet has an overabundance of carbohydrates and the cheaper proteins, which the body stores as fat.

Cats may also become obese if their diet is too rich in fats or sugars. Cats fed on all organ meat are usually not only fat but also greasy. It's such a sad thing to see an overweight cat. Not only the drain on the cat's laboring heart, caused by the extra weight, saddens one but also the fact that the cat can't play and therefore the circulation is slower. And what really tears at my heart is to see a cat so overweight that he cannot bend enough to wash and clean himself properly. The suppleness of the cat is as legendary as his cleanliness. It is criminal to allow the cat's body to get into a condition where he cannot reach his own anus to clean it. I cry inside every time the owner of an obese cat says to me, "Oh, well, she's been spayed, that's why" or "He's old and fat, there's nothing we can do." A cat that is properly cared for keeps a beautiful figure his whole life. Truly finicky owners cannot stand to have less than a perfect figure for their cats.

I do not believe in crash diets. When confronted with an obese cat and contrite owners, I explain to the owners that changing to the recommended diet will automatically slim the cat down, albeit very slowly. This will happen because after a few days he won't *want* to eat as much; those missing nutrients he was reaching for will now be amply supplied.

Also, the high quality of the protein has a stick-to-the-ribs effect, which is another reason he will not feel hungry. Coming at the problem from another angle, the fact that you are removing food between meals means that the metabolism will speed up again. The cat will have more energy to play, exercise, and burn up calories.

Usually such owners are eager to do little special things to speed up the weight loss and to make it easier on their cats. I recommend feeding half a cupful of Foods of Nature with two tablespoonfuls of water, a teaspoonful of Vita-Mineral Mix, a teaspoonful of extra bran, and a teaspoonful of finely grated raw carrot. Give half of this in the morning and half at night. If you're using the "I'll-Do-Anything-for-My-cat" Diet, add the carrot and bran to that. The bran and the carrot are the magic ingredients. They make the portion seem like more. The bran raises the quality of the protein, as does the Vita-Mineral Mix. And, because fat cats are inactive, it is logical to assume that the intestinal walls are thick with sludge. The bran and carrot will scrape away the old deposits bit by bit and carry them out with the stool. I caution the owners to provide extra attention to such a cat, not only petting and cuddling but also frequent casual eye and voice contact. If without realizing it you have been teaching your cat that "food is love," you must now introduce him to some of the other delightful ways that love can be expressed. Attention is love, too, you know.

Often a lonely pussycat comes to his owner for attention, and, without thinking, the owner assumes that the cat is asking for food. If your cat is overweight, you may have trained him to do just that. So when he comes to you and cries, distract him with an alternate pleasure. Get out a brown paper bag and throw it on the floor—or roll a ping-pong ball. Or pick him up and hug him. Be sure, too, that you approach him with petting and praise at times when he's not expecting it. The more secure and relaxed he feels, the easier it will be to change the undesirable pattern of his eating habits.

As the weight goes down, everything else will improve. The eyes will be brighter, the fur silkier, the skin pink and clean. It's easier to pick up a lighter cat. When you do, and you snuggle your nose into the ruff, take a good sniff and enjoy the delicate aroma exuded by the furs of a healthy cat. Don't be surprised at the change in temperament. Your cat may well become more gregarious and alert, yet at the same time more mellow—relaxed but not lethargic.

Owners are always surprised when a correction in the diet produces an improvement in temperament. To me, it's only logical. A fat, uncomfortable cat who can't clean his own anus is bound to be nervous, grouchy, and lethargic. I frequently tell such owners that they're wasting their cat. They don't know what a beautiful animal they really have. It's not a matter of creating anything new. You're simply realizing the potential that's already there.

Fasting and Force Feeding

A fully grown cat can fast three to five days without harm. Sometimes it's good to fast your cat for a day. Wild animals fast themselves naturally if they become ill. A sick cat often stops eating. Caution: Do not fast a kitten, an elderly cat, or a diabetic; *and* only fast your cat on a day when you are at home all day and have time to give extra play and love. Never, never, let your cat fast if you are away.

Fasting can be a wonderful tool. It can be used to perk up the appetite of cats who won't eat. If you skip one meal or even two—not even offering food (in other words, don't even let them smell food)—then at the following meal, when you finally do offer food, there is a much better chance that they will eat. That trigger mechanism in the brain that is activated by the smell of food has had a rest. You can raise the odds in your favor even more if the food you finally offer is something absolutely stupendous. I always try broiled chicken thigh. It hasn't failed me yet. But be sure to broil the chicken—canned chicken or chicken boiled in water usually will not work. I've also seen excellent results with baby food chicken, beef, veal, or lamb with one teaspoonful of Vita-Mineral Mix.

Understand that these tempting morsels are not complete nutrition in themselves. As soon as possible, I mix in one part baby food oatmeal and one part vegetable to four parts meat. I also slip in the Vita-Mineral Mix as soon as I can, and some alfalfa sprouts. You can try these ploys before resorting to force feeding.

Force feeding may become necessary if the cat is very thin and sick and if the veterinarian recommends it. But don't be in too much of a hurry to force feed a sick cat. A sick cat just naturally fasts because during a fast energy is turned away from digestion and toward healing.

The main ingredient needed for force feeding is patience. You must make the experience pleasant for the patient. If the cat is thrashing around or nervous, you should wrap him or her in a towel first. (See section on "Wrapping the Cat for Medication" earlier in this chapter.)

Prepare a special food made up of two parts baby food (High Meat Dinner, beef, chicken, or lamb), one part pureed vegetable, and one part baby food oatmeal. Or prepare a mixture from scratch using broiled chicken. Add a teaspoonful of Vita-Mineral Mix and an extra teaspoonful of bran, and use just enough water so it will hold together in tiny balls no bigger than a green pea. Pick up a small amount of the food on your index finger. With your left hand, grasp the cat's cheekbones from above and tilt the head upward. Then, with your right middle finger, pull the lower jaw down while you quickly wipe the morsel off your index finger onto the palate just in back of the upper front teeth. Then let go and allow the cat to swallow several times. You must give ample time for swallowing. As long as the cat continues swallowing motions, don't try to feed the next morsel.

It may take ten to fifteen minutes to get a teaspoonful of food down the cat this way but a teaspoonful is ample for a feeding because a cat sick enough to be force fed needs to be fed only tiny amounts every four hours. Frequent small meals are easier for the stomach to handle. Feeding too large an amount may kill the cat because it takes too much energy to digest it—the stomach can't handle it. If the cat vomits it back up, you've lost everything. And, if the cat is too weak to vomit (vomiting takes quite a bit of energy), the huge amount lies in the stomach—a mass too large to be moved out into the intestine by the weakened cat. The food then acts like a block, which prevents any further nourishment, so the cat dies. Don't feed more often than every three or four hours. You must allow the stomach time to digest and process the food.

Force feeding liquids can be dangerous. One false move, and you may choke the cat by dribbling the liquid near the windpipe during an inhalation. If you need to give liquid medications or vitamin supplements and you must force feed a liquid, go slowly. You begin as in force feeding, by tilting the cat's head back slightly, lifting up on the cheekbones from above with the left hand. Then, instead of opening the cat's mouth at all, you insert the tip of the dropper into the corner of the mouth, slipping it between the teeth and the cheek pouch. If the cat's head and the dropper are tilted at the proper angle, any liquid coming out of the dropper will dribble from the cheek pouch down the side of the cat's throat. The cat will feel the liquid in the cheek pouch and automatically alter the breath pattern so as not to inhale while the liquid is in the throat. Be careful—if the head is tilted too far back, the cat can't swallow and may still inhale the liquid and choke. Also, if you squirt too fast you could drown the cat. If you try to empty the whole dropperful in one squirt, I'll guarantee you that three-quarters of it will come out again. The proper method is slow, gentle pulses, one after the other, partially depressing the bulb of the dropper more and more each time. Be aware of the cat's swallowing rhythm and take your rhythm from that: for example, squirt, swallow, swallow; squirt, swallow, swallow.

Always wipe the cat's mouth when you finish—it's so much easier to wipe off food and liquid while it's still fresh and wet. Fur messy with old, dried food is terribly depressing as well as unsanitary.

It is not good to have a litter box near the sleeping area (see Chapter 3), but in the case of a convalescing cat an exception might be made in order to make it easier for the patient. Be extra finicky about keeping it clean.

Exercise is also important. The only way to get the circulation to improve is to get the cat to exert himself a little bit. So, when the cat's health allows, urge the cat to get some exercise by carrying him down the hallway a bit and letting him walk back to his bed.

Pilling

The easiest way to give a cat a pill is to kneel down on the floor, with your knees apart and your feet together in back. Back the cat in toward you. Have the pill ready beside you. With your left hand, grasp the cat's cheekbones from above and tilt the head back. Hold the pill between the index finger and thumb of the right hand. Using the middle finger, pry the lower jaw down by inserting the fingernail between the cat's teeth. Then pop the pill far back down the throat—beyond the hump in the tongue. Let go suddenly, so the cat will swallow with surprise.

Some people like to massage the throat down in a swallowing motion. This is fine, but remember, once the pill is in the cat's mouth don't continue to hold the head back with the nose pointing up and don't hold the mouth shut—you will actually be preventing the cat from swallowing. No cat can swallow with the throat all stretched out.

Like so many other things, pilling becomes easier the more you do it. Dr. Rowan preferred to throw the pill down the throat in a lovely little arc. He also had a way of lightly blowing into the cat's nostrils to make the cat open his or her mouth. He had developed "pilling" to a fine art.

I found that my own art developed between my trying to teach the cat how to take a pill and the cat trying to teach me how best to give it. I think with this attitude you will definitely progress. With some cats, I use the index finger of my right hand to shove the pill over the tongue hump toward the throat opening. I keep the nail on this finger so short it is practically nonexistent. You cannot use this method if you have anything but the shortest of nails. A nail could scrape against the roof of the cat's mouth, and the mucous membrane is very delicate back there. Don't make the mistake of holding the cat's mouth closed. Cats swallow with their teeth ajar, and the tongue must be able to move out through the front of the lips. In fact, you can tell that the cat has swallowed by watching for the appearance of the little pink tongue flicking out and in.

Before you try to pill cats, find out from your vet if it's all right if they take the pill with food, because some pills must be given before the meal. If it is OK to put the pill in the food, I suggest you use the method I worked out when Ruth Vollbracht was boarded with me while she convalesced from a liver infection. I had to make sure she took all of the medication and didn't just eat around it. I delayed the dinner and then took an unusually long time preparing the meal so Ruth smelled the food but could not get at it. She started to drool, and her hunger became even sharper. I crushed the pill and divided it into two or three sections (depending on the size of the pill). Then I took a quarter teaspoonful of food and hid a part of the pill inside it. I held the bit of food with the pill inside just out of Ruth's reach and asked her if she'd like to have it. If she reached for it, I gratified her. I gave it to her with lots of love and encouragement. This way she wolfed that little bit down, never noticing the piece of pill hidden inside.

Now I pretended that that's all I was going to give Ruth. I started making my own salad. When she asked for more to eat, I appeared surprised that she was still hungry and repeated the process of holding the tidbit concealing the pill, asking her if she was quite, quite sure she still wanted it. Then again I relented and gave it to her with more gushes of love. Once the pill was consumed, I placed the rest of the dinner in the dish on the floor as usual. I didn't mix the pill in with all of the dinner because that might have been just the day that Ruth decided not to finish it. I had to remain in control of those bits of pill until they passed safely down Ruth's gullet.

If this doesn't work for you, you can try the exact same ritual except that, instead of hiding the pill in quarter-teaspoonfuls of your cat's usual dinner, you can mix it with a small amount of some fabulous treat that your cat is sure to gobble up if he gets the slightest chance—baby food lamb, or perhaps a small piece of sardine if you're desperate—but don't stoop to tuna, that's really beyond the pale. Sometimes even this won't work, and you'll have to pill the cat in the classic manner described earlier, or after wrapping the cat in a towel. Or you can mix the crushed pill with baby food meat and bit by bit wipe it off near the back of the front teeth, as in force feeding.

Liquid Medication

As with force feeding liquids, with liquid medication you must be careful not to choke the cat by suddenly shooting a stream down the center of the throat. Proceed in exactly the same way that you force feed a liquid, as discussed earlier in this chapter. Insert the dropper at the corner of the mouth, sliding it back between the cheek pouch and teeth and releasing the medication in four or five gentle spurts so that the volume of the liquid is small enough each time for the cat to deal with—not all at once. This gives the cat ample time to swallow and also assures that the liquid will dribble down the side of the throat—not go gushing down the middle.

Eye Medication

Position the cat the same way you do with simple pilling—kneel on the floor and back the cat in between your knees, making sure your feet are together so the cat won't slip out behind you.

Begin stroking the head and the throat—you know your cat's favorite places. Eye medication is usually a salve in a tube. Put a dot of the salve on the tip of your right index finger. (Once again, be sure your nail is short.) Continue stroking the cat's head with your left thumb. Now you want to indicate to the cat that you're going to do something to the right eye. You want him to close his right eye. Stroke ever so lightly near and around the eye. Be soothing. The cat will close the eye. As soon as he does so, stroke lightly and gently over the closed eye from nose to cheek several times, making loving, murmuring sounds.

Position that right index finger against the lower lid so that the dot of salve can be pressed against the pupil by simply rotating the finger inward. Don't do it yet. The eye is still closed—you are still stroking with your thumb and murmuring. On one of those thumb strokes, stop mid-way, place the thumb on the upper lid just above the eye slit, pull the lid upward to separate it (slightly exposing the eyeball), rotate your right finger inward, and wipe the salve off on the inside of the lower lid. Then immediately release the thumb, letting the eye close and stroke the forehead a few times. You repeat with the opposite hands for the other eye—put the salve on the left index finger for the left eye. Dr. Camuti, the famous cat doctor, always medicates both eyes. He reasons that, because cats will always scratch the eye that was treated, you should treat both to create confusion.

Keep all your motions very small. Always move in from the back of the head toward the eye. If your cat sees you poking your finger at him from in front, he will naturally try to avoid it by turning his head and wiggling away. It's a reflex action. Humans have the same reflex.

The whole process is really quite pleasant and tranquil. Smearing the dot of salve inside the lower lid is one of those things that cats can place under the catch-all heading of bizarre but harmless human behavior that a loving cat learns to accept and forgive.

Ear Problems

Just as cats' sense of smell is so many times greater than ours, so are the ears much more sensitive. The sign of something wrong with the cat's ears is not always wax or discharge, although those are the most common signs. Any sort of irritation inside the ear canal, any kind of swelling down there, will first of all cause an itch. The very first sign of trouble is when a cat tries to relieve that unreachable itch by rapidly shaking the head or trying to dig in to the ear with a hind claw. Sometimes sores on the forehead or around the ear are not a sign of trouble where the sores are but are caused by the cat's desperate attempt to reach a maddening itch deep inside the ear canal.

Wax in the ears—or any kind of discharge—can be caused by any one of a number of things. The only course for an owner to pursue is to take the cat to the veterinarian and let the veterinarian determine the cause.

Ear mites are easy to treat and get rid of. This is not to say that ear mites are something that you can mess around with. Ear mites can carry other diseases and parasites. Also, ear mite medication, like worm medication, is extremely harsh and potentially dangerous. Even owners who are not finicky should never try buying something over the counter and treating the cat themselves.

As a general rule, the less you put into the cat's ears, the better. If your cat's ears are clean, pink, and healthy, a finicky owner can determine on a regular basis that they are indeed staying that way by cleaning only the area that can be seen with the naked eye once a week with a sterile Q-tip. If you see a tiny bit of soft brown wax on the Q-tip, don't panic. All cats—in fact, all creatures including you—secrete wax in the ears. The wax traps the dust. If you didn't secrete wax, dust could blow in and lodge near the eardrum acting as a sort of mute. So don't worry about a little wax. It's when there's a lot of wax or, worse, when there's a great deal of hard, blackish-brown wax, that you are allowed a startled reaction and should phone the veterinarian for an appointment. Whatever the diagnosis turns out to be, you will probably be given something—a liquid or salve—to put in the ears.

You may have to wrap your cat in order to be sure that you get the salve into the ear rather than all over the ruff and whiskers. I have often medicated ears by simply kneeling on the floor and backing the cat in between my legs (as described in the section on "Pilling" earlier in this chapter). Here again, take the opportunity to make each step feel good. Remember that the cat's ear canal is itching and burning. Have the salve or dropper open and ready on the table beside you.

First, make your cat feel a little better by stroking the forehead and behind the ear, thus distracting attention away from the discomfort inside the ear and indicating clearly where you're going to be working so it won't be a surprise. Include the ear itself in your gentle stroking. Next, take hold of the ear—but first stroke through that hold position, letting the ear slip through your fingers. Again, it feels good and distracts your cat from the discomfort. While you stroke, look for the hole down which you will drop the salve. Pick up the dropper or tube of salve, and when you have the medicine ready at the tip of the applicator take a last stroke, and now gently hold the ear still (down near the base, don't hold the tip). Insert the tip of the dropper or applicator tube into the hole and press out the prescribed amount of the soothing, healing substance. You are making your cat feel better. Now, withdraw the dropper or tube and swiftly press the hole closed by folding the ear down over it to hold the healing medication inside. Be consciously aware of that soothing cream or liquid trickling down the itching, irritated tissue. If you can bring these facts to your consciousness and tell the cat in an honest way what is happening, the cat will focus on the relief experienced rather than on the strangeness of your current mode of expressing love. It's good to lightly press the ear canal closed from the front and side of the ear. If you very gently massage the area, you can sometimes hear the medicine gurgling around in there, bathing irritated membranes and suffocating the nasty organisms. Tell the cat what you are doing. Finicky owners have very close relationships with their cats and will derive immense satisfaction from the relief they give during an ear treatment.

Now, a word of caution. If you are dealing with mites, the standard medications are always quite harsh. Mitox, for example, which is used only once a week or every ten days (but for six or ten weeks), is quite caustic. So skip the massaging part of the ritual once any mite medication is in the ear. Simply hold the cat's head as still as possible, a little tipped to the side and in a position where the liquid can dribble deep into the ear canal and kill the mites. Don't clean the cat's ears with a Q-tip before medication—you don't want to irritate the mucous membrane inside the ear in any way.

A second word of caution: When dealing with mites be very sure to follow strictly the veterinarian's orders as to how often and how long to repeat the treatment. Mites are like fleas, in that you can't kill the eggs. The veterinarian knows the life cycle of the organism and will gear the treatment so that you catch and kill the little horrors shortly after they hatch and before they can reproduce. When the prescribed time is over, before you heave a sigh of relief, a second test must be made by the veterinarian to see that all signs of the infestation are truly gone.

Does My Cat Have Fleas?

Fleas, like mites, also carry other organisms and parasites within them. They, too, have a life cycle that must be taken into account if you're trying to get rid of them, because you can't kill the eggs. Also, any preparation used must be toxic or it won't kill the fleas. So, even if you're not finicky, don't mess around with the over-the-counter preparations—usually they don't work anyway.

One scratch doth not a flea make. Many skin diseases cause scratching and have nothing to do with fleas. However, by any means don't rule out fleas. I have seen fleas in an air-conditioned, hermetically sealed apartment on the nineteenth floor of a luxury building in the middle of Manhattan. The owners swear there are no other animals on the floor to carry fleas and drop eggs on the hall carpets, so how did Samantha get fleas? I don't know. All I know is how to get rid of them.

If you suspect fleas, groom your cat and save the hair in a nice little pile. Take that hair, spread it out to a thin film, hold it up to the light. If you see little black dots in it, exactly as if someone sprinkled pepper on it, that is flea debris—eggs and excrement. You probably will not see a flea.

If you do not see any flea debris, see if the veterinarian can find out why the cat is scratching. If it's wintertime, the artificial heat in the house may be drying the cat's skin. You should use a humidifier and put open pans of water on the radiator every day. Also give your cat half a teaspoonful of butter every other day. Increase the cod liver oil to three times a week. If dry skin is causing the problem, more oil in the diet is a partial answer. If you have some wheat germ oil, alternate that with the butter instead of using all butter every other day. You might as well strengthen the heart at the same time.

If your cat really does have fleas, the easiest course of action is to take him to the veterinarian. You and the vet together can dust the cat carefully with a veterinary flea preparation. Because the life cycle of the flea is ten days long, the dusting should be repeated in nine to ten days.

But that's only half the solution. That debris you saw did not all stay on the cat. There are eggs all over your home—the rugs, the cushions, the bed—in fact, any place where your cat has walked or sat. You can't kill the eggs, as I said. You've got to vacuum them up and then dispose of the bag—not in the wastebasket, where they could easily hatch out and merrily jump out onto the floor—but down the incinerator. Burn them. Or tie them securely in a plastic garbage bag and place it out by the curb, far away from you and the cat. Do this every single day. I know it's a drag, but if you are faithful about it now the total length of time during which you have to worry about fleas will be considerably shortened. After all, this is war. It's kill—or be bitten. Any egg you miss will probably hatch out sometime during the ten-day period and jump onto the cat. They prefer cats to humans. If you have several cats, they prefer the oldest or the least healthy of the group. Actually, it's a very good indication of lowered vitality and poor resistance to see which cat seems to get all the fleas. But you must dust all the cats and dogs, or the fleas will simply jump onto the untreated animals.

So then you redust the cat in ten days and hopefully kill the newly hatched fleas before they can lay. And then, just in case, you continue the whole miserable ritual for ten more days, vacuuming and all.

What about flea collars and tags? They're horrible. The chemicals used in flea collars and flea tags are just ghastly. They won't get rid of fleas anyway. Sometimes they can tend to keep fleas off, but there are much much better ways of doing this, both more efficient and certainly safer. I don't know why I even mention flea collars and tags in a book for finicky owners except that they are in common use and finicky owners want to know the scoop on them.

Flea collars eventually destroy the very follicles of the hair around the neck and ruff. On a Persian, this happens rather quickly. And when it happens, the hairs do not grow back. Never. I know a pretty white Persian whose neck is bald. Her ruff, once the pride of the household, is all but gone. It is a sadness every time I groom her to see this beautiful creature so defaced.

Flea tags work about the same as collars but do not destroy the hair follicles. If you're going to use one, first open up the package and let the air get to it for forty-eight hours before attaching it to a standard cat collar. Take it off during the night. Don't leave it on every day, twenty-four hours a day. And give your cat 500 units of vitamin C every day, to help the body deal, at least in a small way, with the toxic fumes the tag exudes.

There are herbal flea collars available now. The main ingredient is oil of pennyroyal (and sometimes eucalyptus as well). Pennyroyal has a rather minty smell that fleas find unbearable. You can make your own herbal flea collar if you get oil of pennyroyal and saturate a pajama drawstring with it. Go to the notions store where they have a good selection of cords and buy some that is cotton and looks as if it will absorb and hold the oil nicely. Drawstring for pajamas is soft, light, and thick enough to be comfortable. You can sew a little buckle on it, or a large snap will do. Resaturate the cord once a week or if it gets wet. And, if you live in the country, certainly if you live south of the Mason-Dixon Line, where there is no freezing weather to kill fleas—or just before you go on vacation with your cat—bathe the cat and put a teaspoonful of oil of pennyroyal into the second shampooing. (See chapter on grooming.)

Finicky owners, take heart. Your cat is almost assuredly an unappetizing morsel for a flea, because (1) fleas tend to go for sickly, old, or run-down cats, and (2) fleas tend to avoid animals whose diet includes yeast, especially brewer's yeast. Also, most finicky owners habitually give a quarter to half a clove of raw garlic once a week to stave off any possible infection, and eating raw garlic causes the body to exude a natural insect repellent. (Yes, it will also work for *you*, in mosquito areas—but the garlic must be raw and fresh).

So, beginning a week before you leave for vacation (or always, if you are in a warm climate where fleas abound) include a little raw garlic in one meal each day. Usually cats will eat it once they are used to it. You can mash up a quarter clove or hide it in a morsel of food as in administering pills (see 'Pilling"). It is also possible to carve a piece in the shape of a pill and pill the cat with the garlic.

Remember, cats belonging to a finicky owner who habitually keeps the quality of nutrition high have a much better chance of remaining free of fleas. Cats on a poor-quality diet who are suddenly getting yeast and garlic will certainly have a better chance but the odds in their favor do not begin to approach the odds in favor of the well-nourished cat.

As a groomer, I have been called to minister to many cats with fleas—matted Persians who have spent the summer romping through the tall sea grass and come home totally infested with three varieties of fleas, nesting under every mat and dropping flea debris everywhere they step. This is certainly a problem for a professional groomer or a veterinarian. I usually do not bathe cats who have fleas until after three 10-day treatment periods have passed. But in cases of matted Persians I first remove the mats, being careful to immediately plunge each piece into a bowl of water, because drowning is the best way to be sure of killing a flea. I then bathe the cat either in the usual manner (see chapter on grooming) or, if the cat will allow it, I begin to fill the sink where the cat is standing very slowly with water so that as much of the cat as possible is immersed. I pour copious amounts of water through the furs. Fleas drown easily. They will all try to escape by running up to the head. Take an extra-fine toothed comb (you can use a delousing comb), comb the refugees out of forehead, cheeks, and chin, and plunge them gleefully into the waiting bowl of water before they can jump away. They'll try to crawl into the cat's eyes, to escape into the corners of the mouth. Slay! slay!—show no mercy!

Once the bath is over and the cat is dry, I do the first of the three

10-day dustings and try one more time to get through to the owner about the virtues of a high-quality diet and bathing with pennyroyal rinse *before* going on vacation.

When the third 10-day period is over, bathe the cat again to get rid of the toxic flea powder. Add a teaspoonful of oil of pennyroyal to three tablespoonfuls of the shampoo solution for the second soaping. The pennyroyal has a nice, minty smell, which will tend to adhere to the furs and act as a flea repellent. Use the herbal flea collar as well, and be sure you are putting garlic and extra brewer's yeast in the food.

Ringworm, Bald Patches, and Other Skin Problems

I have seen ringworm as a tiny little spot on a healthy cat and as extensive areas of baldness on an old or sick cat. I always deal with any fungus or parasitic infestation both topically, with an application on the skin, and systemically, by making sure the quality of the diet is superb. And you can add extra yeast and raw garlic to try to render the body unattractive to the invading organism. You might also apply a strong solution of the herb golden seal to the affected areas. Golden seal can be bought in capsules at a health food store. To make the golden seal solution, heat a quarter cup of water, remove from heat, and empty the contents of the capsule into the water. Let it stand for fifteen to twenty minutes to steep.

Golden seal root extract can also be used. A small bottle costs about $12. It's very concentrated, so you should use only five drops to one teaspoonful of water for ringworm wash. It's much easier to use in this form.

I use a quarter of a cotton ball to apply the solution to the affected areas at least twice a day. Because the cat will probably lick it off, you may want to apply it three or four times a day. And because golden seal lowers blood sugar, you must be sure your cat is eating a normal amount of food.

Ringworm is around us all the time. You and I probably have ringworm spores on our skin right this moment. Athlete's foot is a kind of ringworm. It's a yeast or a fungus. So why don't you and I have ringworm lesions? For the same reason that we don't have a virus cold even though we are constantly breathing those viruses into our body with every breath. We are healthy, our resistance is high, and our acid-alkaline balance is such that our bodies do not make a good home for viruses, germs, and parasitic infestations to take hold. If I see ringworm on a cat, my main concern is not the ringworm. Ringworm can be cured—it's easy. My main concern is to discover what has caused that cat's body to become an acceptable home for fungus. Is the acid-alkaline balance impaired? Has the cat perhaps been eating foods with preservatives or a protein source where the amino acids are not properly balanced? Dry food is a good example of that. Cats who eat dry or semimoist food seem much more prone to pick up fungus and parasitic infestations. Or perhaps someone new was taking care of the cat, and food was left available between meals several days in a row? The resultant slowing of the metabolism could cause the pores to exude an unusual amount of wastes and so change the pH (acid-alkaline) balance of the skin. Any of these things is so easy to correct that I always hope that's what it is.

The other possibility is that the cat is under some sort of stress or the cat's system is currently fighting some other infection somewhere in the body. Perhaps the cat's system will win out in the end, but in the meantime the battle is depleting it and giving the ringworm a chance to take hold. The thing to do, along with your topical application at the site of the ringworm, is to mobilize and arm your cat's body with extra vitamins in addition to the super high quality diet. Now is the time for all those additional supplements you occasionally add to the food. Give the cat a soft-boiled egg three or four times a week. Add one teaspoon of chopped alfalfa sprouts to every single meal and give an extra dose or two of cod liver oil and vitamin E.

Bald patches can be caused by any number of things. Sometimes a cat will try to scratch a mat out of his fur, pull too violently, and end up with a bald patch where some of the hair was torn away. This is not serious. Eventually it grows back in. Poor circulation of the skin due to a heart condition or clogged capillaries can cause thinning hair or bald patches. Allergies can also thin the hair. Many medications cause hair loss, especially on cats eating low-quality diets. Mange is a very rare affliction. I suggest a high-quality diet and a consultation with your vet.

Dr. Perper showed me a young kitten infested with mange mites. The bizarre feature of this particular case was that the kitten maintained a normal coat of hair through it all. The infestation was discovered only because the owner was going through a positive agony of itching. The owner's dermatologist uncovered the cause and suggested that the pet be treated as the source of the problem. Any veterinarian I've ever talked to seems to agree that skin problems are by far the hardest to diagnose.

Acid-Alkaline Swing

I have a little trick I use whenever I get a warning that my cat's body might be battling something. I reason that the invading organism has taken hold either because the cat's body is too alkaline (very rare) or too acid. So I proceed to swing the pendulum from acid to alkaline and back again, in an effort to disturb the attacking organism. I do this by feeding supplements that I know to have an acid-producing effect for two days and feeding other supplements that tend to alkalize on the next two days. I choose specific supplements that have lots of side effects—all of them beneficial.

For the acid day, I use 500 units of natural vitamin C twice on that day. You can get it in the health food store. Choose a formula that states on the label that it also contains bioflavinoids and rutin. Choose a tablet that is long and flattish, like a lozenge, for easy swallowing. I use either C-Hi or Hi-C. Besides acidifying the body, vitamin C acidifies the urine, getting rid of little bits of gravel and helping destroy many germs that can breed in the bladder. It also helps build up the body's immunological response and renders the system better able to deal with stress.

On the alkalizing day, I give crushed garlic. This also protects against parasitic invasion and actually contains a natural raw antibiotic. I sometimes also use kombu seaweed. You can buy it in any health food store—Erewon is a very good and popular brand. Just break off a square inch of the dried kombu, cut, break, or crumble it up into tiny pieces, and soak it in a cup of water for a half hour. Simmer it for another half hour covered. Don't let it boil dry. Let it cool and add this to the food. Don't try to keep it in the refrigerator for more than two days. It is extremely perishable; make it up as you need it. Kombu is full of minerals and contains very little sodium, so it can be used even for heart patients. Use extra alfalfa sprouts on the alkaline day and none on the acid days.

Now is also the time to give multiple vitamin pills more frequently. Instead of just twice a week, give them four or five times a week, usually on an "acid" day. And don't forget the cod liver oil—give it three or four times a week instead of twice.

Be conscious of how much time your cats spend in active play. It will help their circulation greatly if you can get them to join you in some raucous sport at least once a day. If your cat is not the sporting type, you might try to get hold of a peacock feather. Florist's suppliers often have them. These feathers are so irresistible when waved or trailed in front of cats that cat show judges use them to elicit response from blasé pussycats.

Diarrhea and Constipation

Both diarrhea and constipation are treated with bran, because bran is a conditioner. It absorbs and holds liquid. So, if you are dealing with diarrhea add between a half and one teaspoonful of extra bran to each meal (depending on the size of the cat). The bran will absorb the wateryness—it will turn a watery stool into a stool of soupy or mashed potatoes consistency. If the stool is too hard and the cat is constipated (the cat should pass one or, ideally, two stools a day), mix a half to a full teaspoonful of bran into each meal plus an extra tablespoonful or so of water. The bran will tend to "plump up" the stool—soften it. It will carry the moisture with it and maintain the moisture in the stool all the way through the intestine.

Frequently when cats are sick owners call to ask me what to do about the additional problem of constipation. I realize that a sick cat often stops eating, and the desperate owner tempts the cat to eat by offering baby food meat. This usually works. But, beside the fact that baby food meat is incomplete nutrition, having no grain or vegetable with that finely pureed meat, it is such a low-bulk food that it frequently forms a gluelike substance or a hard little ball in the cat's intestine. This happens because there is no roughage whatsoever for the intestine to "grab onto." If this has already happened, it won't be enough to simply add half a teaspoonful of chopped alfalfa sprouts, a teaspoonful of bran, a teaspoonful of soaked oatmeal flakes, and a teaspoonful of Vita-Mineral Mix to your usual jar of baby food. You should have started out this way in the first place. If that's impossible, you can mix the bran with butter and try to get the cat to eat it that way.

However, if the damage is already done, you'll have to resort to a mucoid. This is another type of conditioner, rather than a laxative, and is not habit forming. Metamucil and Siblin are available over the counter from drugstores. Metamucil is simply a preparation of psyllium seeds ground to a fine powder. These preparations must be taken with large amounts of water because psyllium powder and water together produces a very slippery, mucouslike substance that enables that nasty, hard stool to slide out much more easily. If your cat does not pass a stool for three days, you must call the veterinarian. Anything stronger than Metamucil should have doctor's supervision. If your cat continues to have diarrhea for three days, also call the doctor.

Both constipation and diarrhea are symptoms; they are not diseases in themselves but a sign that something else is very wrong deeper in the body. If the intestinal tract is actually obstructed, chances are that even the vet's laxative won't help. So don't wait more than three days, and make sure the vet knows that it has already been three days since the cat passed a stool. The vet will have to wait an additional day after administering the laxative to see if it works before deciding whether or not an X-ray or enema or even surgery should be resorted to. If the cat's diet is the proper consistency and the cat is groomed every day, such a situation almost never arises.

Kidneys

The kidneys detoxify foreign chemicals and substances such as cigarette smoke and food additives. The kidneys must also eliminate the amino acids (which make up protein) not used by the body. If the cat's diet contains too much protein or a low-quality protein with the amino acids out of balance, the kidneys must rid the body of the excess amino acids.

Symptoms of kidney failure include frequent, copious drinking; frequent, copious urination; pale, watery urine; and periods of lethargy. If the kidneys are failing, make their job as easy as possible by feeding less protein and by making sure that the protein you do feed is only the highest quality and that the amino acids that make up the protein are as perfectly balanced as possible. Because leftover protein is converted to starch, in the diet to aid the kidneys feed more starch and only enough protein to fill the actual daily requirements. It is also best to use only spring water and to eliminate all chemicals from the cat's food and environment. Because all that liquid washing through the system washes away many minerals and B vitamins, the Vita-Mineral Mix should be generously supplied. And because the blood becomes acid, it is also beneficial to include a little ginseng and golden seal in the treatment.

DIET FOR THE CAT WITH KIDNEY PROBLEMS

Water

Spring water, bottled water, or vegetable water; add 1 teaspoonful of ginseng tea or golden seal tea (if the cat refuses to drink the water with the golden seal in it, give 1 dropperful of golden seal tea three or four times a week as a liquid medication)

Basic Carbohydrate Mix

1 cup mashed potatoes (not instant) *or* pureed barley flakes

2 tablespoons Vita-Mineral Mix

2 teaspoons soft butter

Proteins

Lightly broiled chicken or beef *or* Soft-boiled egg or scrambled egg (use *with* other meat, not alone) *or* Baby food chicken *or* Baby food chicken High Meat dinner

- *Each meal should contain*

4 parts carbohydrate mix

1 part protein

1 teaspoon chopped broccoli or other vegetable or vegetable juice

Blend together and store in glass jar.

Supplements

(give each day mixed in food or administer by dropper *after* meal):

½ teaspoon cod liver oil

½ teaspoon wheat germ oil

1 teaspoon Lixotinic (a B vitamins and iron tonic available from the veterinarian)

Because kidney failure usually results in wastes being exuded through the pores of the skin, groom such cats every day and bathe them once a week. This way they will not be recycling their own waste products back into the system when they lick themselves. Encourage exercise so that breathing will deepen and the lungs will rid the body of more carbon dioxide and other wastes in the exhalations.

The Aging Cat

In the aging cat, the assimilation of nutrients is not as efficient as in younger cats. Attack the problem in three ways.

1. *Feed smaller meals more frequently, as a kitten is fed.* My Priscilla, who is 17½, gets three or four meals a day depending on my work schedule. I don't make the mistake of giving large meals in hopes of putting more

weight on her. The object is to have the stomach less than three-quarters full, because its muscular action is not as strong as it was. And, because digestive juices and enzymes are not being as plentifully supplied by her system as before, a small meal will be more efficiently mixed with the digestive juices available.

2. *Supply some additional enzymes and bile.* I give Priscilla one-quarter of a Digestol tablet either in her meal or, more frequently, after the meal crushed up in her favorite dessert of half-and-half and baby food oatmeal. She gets about two teaspoonfuls of this dessert with the quarter tablet, four drops of wheat germ oil (I'd like to give her eight drops but four is all she'll accept), four drops of cod liver oil, and six drops of a vitamin B and iron tonic called Lixotinic (which I get from the veterinarian). The Digestol tablet contains bile and enzymes to augment those produced by her own body.

3. *Make sure that the diet is supplied with a much larger amount of vitamins, because the cat won't assimilate them all anyway.* Use more of the high-powered foods such as cod liver oil, wheat germ oil, alfalfa sprouts, egg, yeast, wheat germ, lecithin—in other words, double the Vita-Mineral Mix. And give a multiple vitamin four times a week instead of twice a week. Cats are naturally heavy meat eaters, and because meat is not a perfectly balanced protein it is not unusual to find that cats over fifteen years old have some percentage of kidney failure. I therefore recommend at least slightly increasing the proportion of carbohydrate and emphasizing the better-balanced proteins. I have completely eliminated all junk food from Priscilla's diet. A young body can process out and dispose of the sugar in half a teaspoonful of Breyer's vanilla ice cream. Now that she's 17½, half-and-half is nicer, and much more chic.

Cystitis and Random Wetting

There are many misconceptions about cystitis. Cystitis is a disease that irritates the bladder and urethra. Irritation in turn causes redness, swelling, itching, and burning. It is first uncomfortable and then painful. In the beginning, the itching and burning irritate the urethra and make such cats think they want to urinate all the time. They will run to the litter box three or four times in one minute; they will squat, perhaps strain. They may pass up to a tablespoonful of urine, or only enough to moisten three pieces of litter—or there may be no urine at all. Cystitis is easiest to treat and cure if it is caught early. So if your cat runs to the litter box two or three times in one hour, take the cat to the veterinarian that very day— better safe than sorry, as always. At this early stage of the disease, when the veterinarian examines the cat, he or she will find that the bladder is small and hard because the urethra is not yet swollen shut and the cat is successfully voiding every drop of moisture as soon as it enters the bladder. If the disease is left untreated, the urethra will swell shut, and the veterinarian will discover a distended, full bladder.

I was caring for George, a dapper black short-hair, while his adored owner was in the hospital. Whenever an owner goes away, I watch the litter box very carefully to be sure the cat is putting out an average amount of urine. I know that cystitis has been proven to be an emotionally triggered disease. Cats who are susceptible to cystitis can go through their whole lives without an attack. But if you subject such cats to emotional stress, especially sadness, they will be prime targets for a cystitis attack. With his owner in the hospital, George mourned. He ate, but without relish, and didn't seem to care whether it was Foods of Nature or chicken thigh on the plate. He'd greet me when I came in to the back room where I kept him, he'd purr politely during our cuddle sessions, but I always detected a sort of sigh under the purr. One day, before the week was out, I noticed that George ran to the litter box three times while I was in the room cleaning up. Alarmed, I too ran to the litter box to find out what the results of his trips had been. There was a little dab of wet litter the size of a split pea.

Cystitis is classified as an emergency. You don't wait. Dr. Perper was on vacation, so I called another doctor who had a fine reputation and scheduled an appointment for George. The veterinarian's examination of George had barely begun when I realized that the veterinarian himself was ill. He was sneezing, his eyes were running, and he looked most uncomfortable. In fact, he looked much worse off than my pussycat.

The examination was the standard palpation of the abdomen with a glance down the throat. When he felt that small, hard bladder, he declared that George was a perfectly healthy cat. I was taken aback—I knew that perfectly healthy cats do not run to the litter box three times in two minutes. They do not put out urine by the dropperful, they do not strain and have worried looks on their faces while squatting. I told the vet a second time about George's litter box behavior. He said again that George was healthy—the bladder was not distended. Then he started blowing his nose again.

I gave up, packed up the cat, and left, wondering if Dr. Perper would be back soon or if I would have to find yet another veterinarian to tell me what to do about these symptoms—someone who wasn't preoccupied with his own illness.

I was giving George all the high-quality protein I could and 500 units of vitamin C twice a day, in an effort to keep the urine acid. I pilled him with raw garlic every day, and I kept running into the back room to administer hugs and kisses to George. He had two nice little females back there with him—my current adoptables—and he seemed to be settling in. But the frantic running to the litter box continued, and his wet spots were now down to the size of a large pinhead.

On Monday Dr. Perper was back. He diagnosed George as having cystitis so quickly and unhesitatingly that I asked him if George's bladder was now distended. This is when I learned about the early stages of cystitis. Dr. Perper explained that at the early stage of the disease the irritation caused the bladder to urinate frequently so that the bladder is bound to be empty, which means that it will feel small and hard. Thank heavens George was still in that early stage. He was put on antibiotics and acidifiers. And now that I was armed with a diagnosis and medical treatment, I could relax and dig in to begin my own work of nutritional support specifically tailored to the needs of my fuzzy friend.

George did not get any worse over the next week, but he did not respond at all, as far as I could see, to the antibiotics that he swallowed so politely three times a day. I was also giving him acidophilus culture as a nutritional support for the antibiotics. He was supposed to take the antibiotics for five days. On the fourth day, I called Dr. Perper, gave him my observations that the antibiotic was not having any effect, and was told to drop by the office and pick up a different antibiotic.

When I asked him if we could substitute vitamin C for the little purple acidifier pills, he agreed but cautioned me to make the change only if George was eating normally. He said the new antibiotic sometimes killed the appetite and caused diarrhea. That's why he had tried the other antibiotic first. I told him I would give George even more acidophilus in hopes of controlling the diarrhea. "Good luck," he said, and I wondered if he meant any more than he was saying. For the next five days, I watched George's appetite dwindle until I finally commenced partial force feeding in order to be able to use the vitamin C. I watched him pass three black, runny, evil-smelling stools a day and realized what Dr. Perper must have been thinking when he wished me good luck with the new antibiotic. George became visibly thinner but he did stop running to the litter box. He smiled more often and became affectionate with "the girls" in his room.

The third day I made a call to Dr. Perper at the office to give a progress report. I needed reassurance because of that horrible stool. He assured me that it was normal with this medication and that, from the sound of it, George was responding beautifully. He told me to finish the course of the drug. I must say I couldn't wait to finish the drug and be rid of the accompanying side effects. That sweet animal took anything and everything I chose to shove down his throat. I wanted nothing more than to see him healthy, comfortable, plump, and carefree as he deserved. It's very hard not to fall in love with a cat to whom you are giving nursing care.

George is in great shape now. I continued the acidophilus in his food for two weeks after the antibiotic and cystitis were gone. His owner told me that he had never had cystitis before, but now that we know he has the tendency I watch his food intake like a hawk. His menu always contains very high quality protein to keep his urine acid so that cystitis germs cannot thrive. All the other nutrients are generously supplied, to keep his general resistance high. And George gets 500 units of vitamin C every day, because we now know that despite his loving and jaunty air he is quite sensitive to stress.

There is a popular misconception that cystitis is only a disease of male cats. This is not true. I've known of many female cats who have suffered from cystitis. And I've met many people who know that dry food in the diet can bring on an attack of cystitis and who still feed dry food to their female cat simply because she is a female and they think that therefore she's immune. My own Priscilla was a victim of that sort of thinking before she came to me. Fortunately she's got a constitution like cast iron, dainty and delicate as she may appear.

If your cat should begin the frequent litter box syndrome, be it male or female, move fast and get the cat to the veterinarian. But also pop in 500 units of vitamin C. Vitamin C is one of those things I keep available at all times.

George was a lucky cat. Cystitis ends in a horrible death, and it happens all too frequently because it is such a quiet disease. There is no vomiting, no fits, no foaming at the mouth. There can be blood in the urine but this is usually not noticed in the litter box. Usually that pitiful running back and forth to the litter box is the only apparent symptom,

Sometimes the cat starts random wetting during the early stages of cystitis. Several times owners have called me to ask what to do because their cat has suddenly begun random wetting all over the house. They usually tell me that, in their opinion, their cat is trying to punish them for being away from home an unusual amount of time or for changing the brand of food or because they had a baby. I always advise such people to have their veterinarian check first of all for cystitis. Then I explain that there is a fine distinction here. Yes, a cat may wet outside the box because you were gone too long, but cats do not use urination to express anger or dismay. Wetting outside the box is probably more distressing to the cat than to you. Here's what really happens: A stress situation results from your being away, or having the baby, or whatever. The stress target area in this particular cat is the urinary tract. The cat's urethra starts reacting by swelling, itching, and burning, so he or she has a spasm and the urine comes out then and there—whether the cat likes it or not. The stress situation triggered it, but your cat certainly didn't plan it. Random wetting is so against the cat's nature that I always insist that there is some cause that has nothing to do with the cat's making a conscious statement. The prohibition against drawing predators to the area because of the urine smell is far too basic.

By far the most likely explanation for the random wetting is that during that early stage of cystitis that irritation and itching in the urethra forced the cat to squat wherever he happened to be. As a precaution and, more important, as a convenience to your pussycat to make things easier during a dreadful and painful disease, put at least one litter box in each and every room that your pet frequents. Your cat will bless you for it because when he's got to go, he's got to go.

Another consideration, with this disease especially, is warmth. A wonderful assistant, Maria, who is no longer with me, told me that she had once suffered from cystitis. What a valuable contribution she made to my knowledge of how to deal with pussycats suffering from that same disease! She said she always felt terribly cold. She could just never get warm enough and shivered uncontrollably under piles of blankets. She felt sick but could not throw up. So now I always provide a padded and protected resting place with a hot water bottle in it for a cystitis cat. I generally use a cardboard box laying on its side with a folded towel inside and another towel draped across the top and partially covering the opening to keep out drafts and hold in the heat.

If this disease is left untreated and blockage occurs, the bladder swells with urine. The cat will begin to first whimper, then cry out, and then scream with pain while crouching in the litter box, unable to pass one single drop of that filthy bloating fluid through the urethra, which is now swollen shut. If you call the veterinarian at this stage, he or she will undoubtedly tell you to drop everything and come at once. Dr. Perper and Dr. Kepner at the Feline Health Clinic will come charging over to the clinic even in the middle of the night. The cat must be catheterized at once. The backup of poisons caused by the retention of the urine can kill the cat in a matter of hours.

Catheterization is painful and must be done under anesthetic, which is not only dangerous but a drain on the cat's system. Catheterization almost always causes bladder infection, which must be treated along with the cystitis infection. It's the usual side effect, and veterinarians know they have to deal with it. I always give 200 units of vitamin E a day during the catheterization and 100 units a day for two weeks afterward to minimize scarring. In other words, treat this as an operation. I use the same supplements—vitamins A, D, E, and C. A and D support the metabolism, E minimizes scarring and supports the heart, and C acidifies the urine, cushions the effects of stress and anesthetization, and fights infection.

Because cystitis is affected by emotions, hospital visits by the owner are of paramount importance. Such visits are always important, but with cystitis those visits are crucial. And once the cat is treated, the bladder emptied, antibiotics administered, and the disease controlled, the diet must be improved and the emotional environment altered to prevent a repeat performance.

If the diet is not improved, or if the cat remains distressed, insecure, or unhappy and attacks recur, there comes a time when further catheterization is no longer possible. Too much scarring has occurred already. At this point, many cats are euthanized (put to sleep) rather than let them suffer while the poisons build up and permeate their entire body, bringing a horribly slow and painful death. The alternative at this stage is an operation called a *urethrostomy,* which some vets perform and some vets do not. It is major surgery, and it is rarely done. One of the finest and most competent vets I have ever known always referred urethrostomies to a colleague of his who was well known for performing that particular surgery especially well. The average vet does not get much practice in doing this operation—thank heavens. It involves surgically removing the urethra and widening the opening from the bladder. I have known several cats who had this surgery and did very well afterward. Of course, all of them were maintained on a very high quality diet and were given a lot of conscious physical affection. For you who read this book, a situation requiring this surgery could almost never arise. You will know the early symptoms, and your cats will be treated and then protected for the rest of their lives. The only way such a situation could arise in your life is if you fall heir to a pussycat who is already in trouble, or if you become aware of a pussycat belonging to a neighbor or friend who is exhibiting symptoms that are quite obvious to you even though the owner doesn't realize the import of what was going on. (One of the most pleasant dividends of being a finicky owner comes on those rare occasions when an opportunity presents itself to help pussycats in distress. I find those times especially satisfying when the pussycats are strangers to me and fate has wafted me in on a tangent to touch them ever so briefly and change the course of their lives for the better. Then I never see them again.)

Teeth and Gums

Cats develop tartar on their teeth just as you and I do. And, like you and I, some produce more tartar than others, and some produce tartar that is soft and can be flicked off with a fingernail, while others, like my Priscilla, produce tartar that resembles granite. It amazes me how often I find tartar-covered teeth on the cats I groom. I always check the teeth and gums at the end of the grooming, especially on new clients. What really surprises me is when I find tartar coating the teeth of a cat who has just been to the veterinarian for a yearly shot and exam. Either the veterinarian's examination leaves much to be desired or, if he or she indeed saw the tartar and didn't suggest doing anything about it, that veterinarian's standards for feline oral health are way below par.

Tartar leads to inflamed, infected gums and holds germs. Germs make the mouth smell bad. (I've often seen Dr. Perper open a cat's mouth, put his nose up to it, and sniff.) Germs and infection in the mouth can lead to infection in the nose, throat, and upper respiratory tract or, at the other end, in the anal glands.

When I see tartar on the teeth, I always try to flick off a nice big piece with my thumbnail and show it to the owner. I then invite the owner to examine the cat's gum while I open the mouth and lift the lip. I point out the inflammation at the gum line, and I explain that this hurts. Mouth pain can make a cat nervous and irritable. Because eating hurts, this is frequently why a cat is off his food and getting thin. New clients often respond that they have been giving dry food every day, so they can't understand why the teeth are not in perfect condition. *Dry food does not clean the teeth.* It never has, and it never will. Even the dry food companies have never claimed that dry food cleans the teeth. As I said in Chapter 2, cats fed an exclusive dry food diet for years frequently have the worst tartar in the world. Dry food can exercise the teeth, and tooth exercise is also important. But, because dry food has so many drawbacks—high ash, low protein quality, abundance of poisonous chemicals—it is much more rational to provide other substances for tooth exercise that have only beneficial side effects and no drawbacks. As discussed in Chapter 2, in the section "Acceptable Crunchies," I prefer such things as brewer's yeast tablets and broiled chicken neck vertebrae.

Whether or not I am able to get some of the tartar off the cat's tooth with my thumbnail, I always recommend a visit to a veterinarian who has higher standards, who will make a really thorough and complete examination. If the condition of the mouth was passed over, one wonders what else might also have been passed over as being insignificant. Dentistry can then be scheduled. I recommend that owners give 500 units of vitamin C on the two days preceding the dentistry and two days afterward, to cushion the effects of the anesthetic. Follow the usual procedure for caring for the cat in the hospital and after arriving home (see Chapter 8, "Going to the Vet).

If I find that the red gums persist as often happens with cats who have been for many months on a low-quality diet, I have good results using the acid-alkaline swing, which I also use when treating fungus and parasites (see the section on "Ringworm, Bald Patches, and Skin Problems" in this chapter). I'm fighting in the dark, because I don't know the cause of inflamed gums, and none of the veterinarians I've talked to seem to know, either.

The first time I tried the acid-alkaline swing on a cat with inflamed gums, I figured it couldn't hurt, because all the side effects are beneficial anyway. We found that when the cat was given 500 units of vitamin C two times a day on the acid days and a third of a clove of crushed raw garlic twice a day on the alkaline days, the inflammation nearly disappeared. I have had even better results when I added the kombu seaweed on the alkaline day. I have seen red and swollen gums respond immediately to treatment with cortisone. However, the response lasts only as long as the cortisone is being taken. In other words, cortisone does not cure but only masks the symptoms. Cortisone, as everyone agrees, is very hard on the cat's system, throwing it completely out of balance and robbing it of several nutrients.

The persistent swollen gum problem is very prevalent in New York City. I can attest to that, and I am still working on the problem at this writing. Under Dr. Pitcairn's guidance, I am trying a treatment with golden seal herb on my own Priscilla and a few old clients. My own feeling is that this, like everything else, is simply a weakness a particular cat has that bubbles to the surface and explodes when the diet is not only low in quality but also laced with too many artificial colors, artificial flavors, artificial scents, and poison chemicals used as preservatives. I have discussed the problem of inflamed gums at great length with four different veterinarians. Every one of them, just like me, was still in the process of tracing down the cause; and, every one of them, just like me, had a pet theory about possible cause and most effective cure. The cures ranged from giving vitamin C to maintaining the cat on cortisone and, in one case, surgically removing the inflamed area of gum.

The only thing you can do in an unclear situation is to give the cat's health all the support you can. Perfect health is a body's natural state. It is a rule of nature that the body will proceed toward perfect health, and all we can do is give it all the support we can in the form of every nutrient it might need to build that perfect health that is its natural state.

Worms

The four most common intestinal parasites are roundworm, hookworm, tapeworm, and coccidia. It's hard to tell which kind of worms a cat has. You have to take the stool to the veterinarian and let him or her examine it under the microscope. Do not buy any kind of worming preparations over the counter. Standard worming preparations are all poison, and you must be very careful how they are used. Worming should be supervised by the veterinarian.

Symptoms exhibited by cats infested with worms are many and varied—loss of appetite, as well as voracious appetite; a big, fat, distended abdomen, as well as weight loss and a bony appearance. Usually the coat gets dull, and there may be hair loss, but not necessarily. Sometimes, in the case of tapeworms, you can see egg sacs in the stool or around the anus. They are about the size of a sesame seed, they are white, and they sometimes move in a maggotlike fashion. If your cat drags the anus along the carpet, this could be a sign of worms or an impacted anal gland. Constant licking of the anal area is a sign that something is definitely wrong, and you should have the doctor check it. That's one of those symptoms that would probably go unnoticed by any except a finicky owner.

If worms are diagnosed, there are two ways that you can handle the problem. In most cases, the best plan is to let the doctor give you the medication to administer, with specific instructions about fasting a number of hours before the medication is given and further instructions about what the first full meal should consist of. He or she may also prescribe a laxative. Under certain circumstances, the doctor may advise that the cat be hospitalized because the cat may vomit and the veterinarian may want to be sure that the medication stays in the cat to do the job.

The other choice is to get a copy of the April 1980 issue of *Prevention* magazine and read Dr. Pitcairn's article on herbal worming and follow his instructions about using herbs as a vermifuge.

I did this with my Big Purr, who had tapeworms. Ironically, I discovered the worms the very day I received my issue of *Prevention* in the mail. I had been horrified to see those awful wiggly, maggoty things in his stool. Gingerly I sliced off a chunk, dropped it into a plastic baggie, and, sealing it very tightly, dropped that into *another* baggie and left it in the refrigerator until I was ready to leave. Purr seemed healthy as a horse, pert and chipper as ever, so I knew that this was not an emergency situation. I dropped off the stool sample at Dr. Perper's, saying that I suspected it was tapeworm. Vinnie, the technician, agreed even before he examined it under the microscope. The evidence of tapeworm was quite obvious. Of course, he took a fecal smear for microscopic examination anyway, in order to find out if anything else was going on.

Tapeworms are carried by fleas, but Purr has no fleas; I asked Dr. Perper where in the world Purr could have picked up tapeworms. He said that they could have been lying dormant in the intestine for years. I remembered that Dr. Pitcairn's article mentioned that most animals have a few worms in their intestines and that the worms contribute in some way to the manufacture or stimulation of certain substances that are part of the immunological response. Evidently, for some reason Purr's intestines became an ideal place for tapeworms to thrive. They became fruitful and multiplied. I told Dr. Perper about Dr. Pitcairn's article and his detailed instructions on how to worm a cat or dog without using chemical poisons. Dr. Pitcairn had mentioned that if the herbal worming does not work nothing is lost, because you can always have the veterinarian give the standard chemical treatment afterward.

I wanted to find out from Dr. Perper if he agreed that it would do no harm to try the herbal remedy along with the fasting and herbal laxatives that Dr. Pitcairn recommended. Dr. Perper was both enthusiastic and curious. He agreed that I should give it a try and requested that I let him know how it worked out. So I went through the whole procedure. It took about a week. The hard part was not stuffing powdered herbs and wet, gooey, crushed garlic into empty gelatin capsules or even tracking down a pharmacy that could supply such esoteric ingredients as wormwood and powdered rue. The hardest part was keeping myself from feeding Purr during the fast days. Purr was several ounces overweight, and I knew it. That fast did him a world of good, and he took it very well. Even though I knew that what I was doing was really great for him in every way, still I found it very, very hard not to feed him. It certainly made me understand the "food is love" syndrome that many owners fall victim to. I'm not going to give you the instructions for herbal worming because Dr. Pitcairn has done it so well and you can easily get a back copy of the April 1980 issue of *Prevention* at the library or by writing to *Prevention* magazine. (*Prevention,* 33 East Minor Street, Emmaus, Pennsylvania 18049).

I waited a couple of weeks after it was over, examining Purr's stool every morning for signs of wiggly, maggoty things. When everything still remained normal looking, I told Dr. Perper that the herbal worming seemed to have worked. It's been over four months at this writing, and I'm still examining all the cats' stools, and so far, so good—it looks like we won.

The herbal remedy is more trouble but the side effects are all beneficial. A fast of a couple of days renews the cat's youth. The backlog of wastes and toxins in the system is cleaned and flushed out. Purr was much more playful and jaunty after the experience. I would recommend the herbal worming to any owners who are able to give pills to their cat. If we can avoid giving poisonous chemicals simply by spending some extra time, I think that it is a very small price to pay, because it results in huge dividends in health for the cat.

Respiratory Ailments

Respiratory ailments can range anywhere from a sniffle at the tip of the nostrils to congestion in the bronchial tubes or the lungs. Often the first symptom is a change in the eyes, which become runny. In the worst stages, the lungs fill up with fluid so that the cat drowns. A veterinarian can relieve this condition by tapping the lungs.

Respiratory infections frighten me, and if I hear a cough or a juicy sniffle I run straight to the veterinarian. As with all ailments, an ounce of prevention is worth two in the bush. If any cat in the house exhibits respiratory symptoms, I dose the whole lot with garlic and commence the acid-alkaline swing (as described earlier in this chapter) for six to eight days.

Repeated respiratory infections indicate that something is amiss. For some reason, germs or viruses are finding it easy to take hold and multiply. Check the teeth. Tartar and filth in the mouth create an excellent breeding ground for germs.

When I hear a sneeze or a cough, I respond in the same way that I do with diarrhea. I immediately begin to watch for any other symptoms—runny eyes, change in the stool, appetite loss, listlessness. If the sneezing or coughing continues for more than two days, I let the doctor check it out. This is like any other disease in a feline. The earlier you catch it, the easier it is to cure.

Repeated Infections

If a cat seems to be forever coming down with something—first a cold, then an intestinal bug, then an eye inflammation or whatever—this is a sign that there is something very much amiss in the basic body functions, and deeper diagnosis is required. The veterinarian will probably request that you let him or her run some blood tests and perhaps take some X-rays or an EKG. This is exactly what happened to sweet-tempered Apollo Kulp. After four successive and random infections, Apollo became short-tempered. He began growling at his companions and sulking in corners. Dr. Perper suspected feline leukemia or some other blood disease. Happily, the tests came back negative for leukemia but revealed liver inflammation, which explained Apollo's low resistance. Once the liver was treated and healed, skinny, lethargic Apollo gained weight and became his old easy-going self again.

Going to the Vet

Finicky owners are as choosy about their pet's medical needs as they are about their own. You never know when an emergency will come up, so it's important to know the symptoms of illness and to have a competent and caring veterinarian who knows your cat's medical history.

When Do You Need the Veterinarian?

"The most common cause of feline death is people bringing the cat to the veterinarian too late." Every veterinarian I know has said these words to me at one time or another. It's not because the owners are careless, it's just that it is very hard to spot the early symptoms of disease in the cat.

Cats accept pain and discomfort in their bodies just as they accept rainfall or a cold day. They assume there's nothing to be done, so they make the best of it and try to carry on as usual. Because they don't cry or moan or fall down, the average owners are completely in the dark about their pet's deteriorating health until the condition becomes so acute that the cat is too weak to rise and gasping for breath.

The case of Daphne comes to mind. Daphne, a tortoise-shell Persian, was a perky little number recently adopted by Carlota Harris as a friend for her charming female Rags. Carlota is an extremely finicky owner and one of my oldest clients. I placed Daphne with her partly because I hoped that Daphne's jaunty, devil-may-care attitude might serve as a bit of a tranquilizer for this very sweet but rather high-strung and overprotective owner. I had had Daphne examined by Dr. Perper just before I turned her over to Carlota. At the time, Daphne had an intestinal bug, which was medicated and cleared up in less than a week. I groomed her on two occasions during the next four weeks, and Louise, my assistant, cat sat while Carlota went out of town for three days, so Daphne did not lack for expert observers. She was flirty and playful and ate like a horse the whole time.

After Carlota came back, I was surprised when she called to tell me that Daphne hadn't passed a stool for two days and asked me if I thought she should take her in to the veterinarian. Ordinarily I would have said no and simply had her triple the bran and add water to Daphne's food and then call me again the next day. But I remembered Daphne's recent intestinal virus, and I knew that Carlota would continue to worry and pass that tension on to both cats. So I told her to make an appointment with Dr. Perper and take Daphne in right away.

During the course of the examination, Carlota mentioned to Dr. Perper that she noticed that Daphne made a funny little noise when she breathed. Dr. Perper listened with the stethoscope, and then he listened again—and again. Then he took an X-ray. Sweet, playful, flirty Daphne had pneumonia. Her lungs were full of fluid, and she had a temperature of 104.5°F (normal cat temperature is 101°F).

Daphne is feeling fine and healthy now, thanks to Dr. Perper's diagnosis and medication and to Carlota's finicky, overprotective ways and devoted nursing care. The point of this narrative is that Daphne's pneumonia was discovered almost by accident. If she hadn't had constipation, she might have been allowed to continue to "breathe funny" until her lungs were so full of fluid that she couldn't breathe at all. After all, Dr. Perper had seen her four weeks before, and both Louise and I had seen her in the intervening time. Because she didn't act sick, we didn't suspect that she was.

The best advice I can give to an owner is this: Any change in your cat's usual behavior patterns should be carefully watched. If it persists or if two or three questionable changes occur, have the veterinarian check it out. Remember, cats don't know that you have the power to make them better, so they are not going to come and tell you if something feels bad. But don't worry and dwell on all the negative possibilities. There is no one better equipped than you, the loving owner, to spot little behavior changes that could spell trouble and correct them long before they become serious.

Of course, the annual visit to the veterinarian for shots and a complete examination is wonderfully reassuring and sometimes uncovers a small trouble before it becomes serious. Over the past nine years, many loving owners have told me stories about taking a beloved animal to the veterinarian for no better reason than "She looked worried to me." In every single case, the owner was right, and illness of one sort or another was diagnosed and treated. Here is a list of some signs of trouble that may help you judge when your cat needs professional help. Remember, it could be nothing—unless the symptom persists or more than one symptom is present:

- *Vomiting.* Usually not serious unless repeated. Cats vomit more frequently than humans, because of their short intestine. Vomiting may be caused by food that is too hot or too cold, eating too much or too fast, or fur balls. However, vomiting may also be a sign of possible heart disease, intestinal blockage, or tumor.

- *Loss of appetite.* Usually not serious. A loss of appetite may stem from the time of year, too much food at the last meal, or a recent snack. However, it may be the result of a low-grade infection, blockage of wastes, rotten teeth, infected gums, hair balls, or stress.

- *Nail biting.* Usually means the cat is just cleaning the nails, but it may be caused by an infection. Check the pads for swelling around the cuticle.

- *Excessive sleeping.* Usually caused by overeating or just the time of year. But excessive sleeping may be caused by an infection anywhere in the body.

- *Coughing.* May be caused by a minor temporary throat irritation or a little something caught in the throat. However, coughing may also be caused by a more serious obstruction in the throat or windpipe, upper respiratory infection, pneumonia, heart ailment, roundworms, or peritonitis, or even rotten teeth.

- *Sneezing.* May be caused by a bit of dust or cigarette smoke. Sneezing may also be caused by the same things that cause coughing, or by an eye infection.

- *Runny eyes or excessive blinking.* May be congenital in Persians, or may be caused by hair in the eye, dirt, or a scratch. But eye problems may also indicate conjunctivitis, upper respiratory infection, infected teeth and gums, or peritonitis.

- *Scratching mouth with claws.* Something may be caught in the teeth, or scratching may be an indication of badly infected gums and rotten teeth.

- *Scratching head with hind foot.* The cat may just be trying to clean the ear, or the scratching may be caused by dry skin. Other possible reasons are fleas, allergy, ringworm, ear mites or, more seriously, an ear infection or a brain tumor.

- *Shaking head.* Usually means itchy ears (see preceding note on scratching head).

- *Tilting head to side.* This may be serious. Tilting the head to the side may be caused by the same things that cause scratching the head, or may be a sign of semicircular canal malfunction or brain tumor.

- *Licking genitals or "scooting" on rug.* Usually means irritation, which may be caused by diarrhea, constipation, worms, parasites, impacted anal glands, or cystitis.

- *Heavy shedding.* May be caused by the time of the year or dry heat in the building. Heavy shedding is also brought on by stress situations, pain, infection, skin disease, allergies, or fleas.

- *Twitching skin.* May be caused by itchy dry skin *or* fleas, heart disease, vitamin E deficiency (steatitis), or a blood clot in the brain.

- *Big appetite in a skinny cat.* Unless found in a growing kitten, this is a symptom of faulty assimilation due to malfunction of a major organ, kidney failure, heart disease, pancreatitis, hyperthyroidism, or liver infection.

- *Unusual nervousness (not wanting to be touched).* May be caused by a change in environment *or* by an infection, pain, waste blockage, or steatitis.

- *Shallow or fast breathing.* Possible causes are heat, stress, fear, fluid in the lungs, abdominal pain, or a tumor.

The following symptoms are more serious and warrant immediate veterinary care:

- *Repeated swallowing.* Usually means an infection or blockage in the esophagus, a tumor, or heart disease.

- *Withdrawing or sitting facing the wall (depression).* Indicates stress or inner tension and is usually a sign of pain.

- *Copious drinking, copious urination, and pale, nonsmelly urine.* Very serious emergency situation—a sure sign of kidney failure.
- *Frequent trips to litter and/or small amount of urine (sometimes blood in urine).* Emergency situation—these are all signs of cystitis.
- *Sitting with head over water dish.* Emergency situation; an indication of very serious illness, usually high fever, often the last state before collapse.

Hopefully a real emergency situation will never arise for you and your cats. After all, they are eating a high-quality diet, which will keep resistance to disease and stress very high. And your annual visit to the veterinarian for shots and checkup will help keep you a jump ahead of any lurking germ.

Now that you have a better idea of when your cats need medical attention, let's examine where you are taking them and look at how you, the owner, can lend your support to enhance and augment the veterinarian's treatment.

The Therapeutic Environment in the Veterinary Clinic

Ask cat owners what their cats do when they are scared, and every time they'll tell you, "They run under the sofa, into the closet, behind the bookshelf, or in back of the bed." *Under, into, behind, in back of*—they hide, they find a safe nook. A high-strung cat will hide out of sight for what seems to us to be the flimsiest of reasons. The mere sound of the doorbell is enough to send some pure-bred types scurrying. Fear of the unknown is the cat's worst fear. To run and hide when frightened is natural to a cat. A declawed cat develops this instinct even more sharply.

Nevertheless, most veterinary clinics lump all small animals together as a group. Those clean, airy, and open cages that are heaven for dogs are a nightmare for cats. Far from providing the secluded nook they crave, everyone can see in and the cats are forced to see out. They are in a constant state of apprehension because of all those new sounds, those strange people doing strange things, and those frightening sharp smells. The cats are trapped, exposed in the open. Caged, they cannot run away, and there is no place to hide. Worse still, in the absence of any other alternative, hospitalized cats often seek the limited shelter provided by the low sides of their litter box. All day and all night they crouch there, tense and ready, expecting to be attacked, adrenalin pumping, vital energy burning away. What a shameful waste! After a few hours of this, cats are worn to such a frazzle that any loud noise or unexpected movement is quite enough to cause spontaneous urination or defecation, which immediately adds one more stress to their already wretched situation. Think how terrified they must be to hide in the litter box. Then add to that the horror of having to smell excrement or urine on themselves.

Some cats are held like that for days. If you were the doctor, how would you like to try anesthetizing a cat in the morning after the cat has spent just one night like that? How would you like to treat a cat in the clinic over a number of days in this stressful situation? If the cat were ill with some disease, what odds would you give for recovery?

Anesthetic is a stress factor that can be isolated—it's a physical thing. Other stresses are no less potent, but unfortunately they are less solid and more difficult for the doctor to isolate, measure, and control. But suppose we could pinpoint and isolate even a few of those additional stresses, then turn them around or simply eradicate them? Think what that would mean in terms of saving the patient's vital energy, calories, and adrenalin. It would widen the margin of safety, raise the percentages in the cat's favor, increase the chances for survival on a borderline case.

Although we cannot change the fact that a hospitalized cat is going to be surrounded by many frightening unknowns, it is a relatively simple matter to cushion the shock and soften the harsh realities. To begin with, lay a large paper bag open in the cage, providing the cat with a little cave—the means of gratifying the instinct to hide. Dr. Rowan sometimes draped a towel over the front of the cage for high-strung cats. In his clinic, soft classical music was played to mute the other noises a bit, and large, healthy plants were hung in every room to add their oxygen to the air. No smoking was allowed, even in the waiting room.

If the veterinarian treats both dogs and cats, it is not unusual to see them mixed indiscriminately in adjoining cages. But stop and think—the great majority of city cats have never even met a dog. Dogs caged at the veterinarian's clinic usually bark and yap—at least some of the time. This is quite normal for a dog. But just imagine poor, terrified Muffy trapped in her small cage. She cannot see the animals who are making those sharp, loud sounds, but they certainly seem close. She doesn't know why the dogs are barking but she assumes that they are after her and that any minute they will succeed in breaking through and into her cage to kill her. She cowers lower into a corner, trembling, ready to fight and die. If

Muffy wasn't ill when she arrived, she certainly will be before she leaves. Her resistance will all be used in fighting stress. To achieve a therapeutic environment, dogs and cats should be housed in separate rooms or, at the very least, on separate sides of the same room, as far away from each other as possible.

In most veterinary clinics and offices, cats are forcibly restrained while medical procedures are performed. The usual method is to firmly hold the cat by the scruff of the neck and the hind feet and stretch the cat out. I know of one veterinarian who was so afraid of being bitten that he insisted that all cats be held like this even for a simple yearly examination. It is a terrifying experience even to watch such a scene. Think of the trauma the cat undergoes. To put it plainly, the cat expects death. "Why else," the cat reasons, "would they hold me this way—stretched vulnerable, unable even to swallow properly?" Again, what a stupid waste of the cat's vital energy. I advise all my clients to insist on being present during all examinations and nonsurgical procedures. At the Cat Practice, Dr. Rowan could do an entire examination, including shots, palpation of the abdomen and anal glands, listening to the heart, clipping the nails, cleaning the ears, taking the temperature—everything—without the cat ever realizing that the exam had even begun. The assistant who held the cat distracted him or her with loving words and expert petting and scratching. Add to this the catnip they always sprinkled on the table at the end of the exam and you can see why (1) cats did not become tense when visiting the Cat Practice and (2) hospitalized cats rallied quicker and recovered easier even after complex procedures. Their energy wasn't wasted.

Many veterinarians use anesthetics for such routine procedures as X-rays and taking blood. Besides being a major stress, however, the anesthetic actually changes the chemistry of the blood that you're trying to analyze. For this reason, more holistically oriented veterinarians simply hold the cat gently but firmly still while doing these tests.

You can spot the holistically aware veterinarian by studying the assistants and technicians in his or her office. If a therapeutic environment is being maintained, they will be trained to respect the cats' physical bodies whether the cats are awake or under anesthetic. After surgery, anesthetized animals will be carried directly back to the comfort of their quiet cages and the security of their paper bags—never left exposed on the cold table or laid aside on the floor until it is convenient for someone to transport them back. An animal will never be lifted—awake or asleep—by the scruff of the neck. Beside the fact that the haunches and pelvis are by far the heaviest part of the animal and therefore must be supported, such action is psychologically damaging to the attitude of respect we are hoping to encourage in the assistant. Lifting cats by the scruff may be only a minor trauma to the cat's body but lifting carefully and with respect is, after all, very easy to do.

In a therapeutic environment, cats are made to feel that they have a say in what happens to them. A greeting is given before they are picked up and handled. Their dignity is preserved by keeping their fur clean. If a liquid medication is accidentally spilled or smeared on the furs of the cat's face or ruff, it is sponged off at once. I have seen fastidious cats distressed by their soiled condition to such an extent that they ripped chunks of fur out by the roots in a desperate attempt to remove spilled medication that has hardened on the hair.

Choosing a Veterinarian

Choosing a veterinarian can be a lot like trying to find a television repairman or a jeweler to fix your watch. Because you know absolutely nothing about television sets and watches, you feel very much at their mercy. Usually all you have to go on is someone else's recommendation. Unfortunately, I have found that most people recommend a veterinarian highly not because they have any rational method of judging, but simply out of psychological need. Their beloved pet's very life may one day be at stake, and they desperately need reassurance that they have indeed chosen rightly. The more people they can get to agree with them and to use the same veterinarian, the more secure they feel. So they go about trying to convince all their friends and neighbors that their veterinarian is the very best and that everyone should use him or her and no one else. Hopefully, after reading this section you will have some more realistic criteria with which to operate. The time to begin searching for a veterinarian is certainly not during a crisis. Begin making inquiries at your leisure, and when you find a new veterinarian you want to try, take the cat in for an examination and the annual shots (if they're due).

If you've got a cat, you want to be sure that your veterinarian knows, understands, and, above all, *likes* cats. When Dr. Rowan left his practice and I found myself without a vet, I went about my search in a sneaky way. I didn't want the veterinarian to be on any kind of good behavior for my benefit that might drop away if the cat was left alone with him.

Vets are generally normal, nice people, like lawyers and schoolteachers, but they are human beings. Some prefer dogs, and some are afraid of cats, and others seem really to believe that cats are second-class citizens after dogs.

So, when I heard that a new cat specialist had opened an office, I took strong, robust, calm Florence for an exam and shots. Feigning ignorance and trying to give a disinterested impression, I said little; I let the vet do all the handling. I just stood and watched but was ready to call a halt if the proceedings were not to my liking. I observed that Dr. Perper greeted Florence by looking into her eyes and using her name—in other words, he established a one-to-one relationship. He treated Florence as an individual, and naturally Florence responded in kind. So, I thought, here we have a doctor who likes cats.

During the examination, which was one of the most thorough I've ever seen, Dr. Perper kept up a running commentary in a calm and soothing tone to inform me, the owner, of what he was doing and why, and what he discovered. Florence was normal all down the line, as I assumed she would be. Of the little mole on her chin, he said just what Dr. Rowan had said—"leave it alone and watch it."

I tend to trust people who take pride in their work, so I asked, with calculated casualness, if I could see where the cats are kept when they stay over. I wanted to give him an opportunity to refuse. He immediately beamed and proceeded to show me not only the cages, which were standard metal but clean, but also the isolation ward, the operating room, and X-ray and cardiogram facilities. Here was a man who was obviously proud of his work.

When your cat is hospitalized, I suggest you make a list of requests as to how your cat is handled, such as (1) doctor and staff announcing their presence before touching the cat, (2) supporting the cats' hindquarters when lifting them, and (3) not leaving an anesthetized cat lying about where he may become chilled after surgery but moving him to a cage with the hot water bottle you will provide.

Veterinarians are people, too; they have morals and standards. Simply look your veterinarian in the eye and calmly explain that you are aware that certain practices of which you disapprove are common in some clinics. Say that, because you have no idea whether any of these things are ever done in his or her hospital, you need to bring these questions out into the open rather than taking anything for granted. That way you won't be shocked or upset just at a time when you need to be giving calm and reassuring vibrations to your cat. If the veterinarian also looks you in the eye and does not get all touchy and insulted but calmly gives you his or her word that your cat will be treated as you wish—specifically on all the points just mentioned—chances are it will be done so.

Visiting Rights

Now, the crucial question—I could never leave my cats in any facility where I could not personally pop in and check on them as often as possible. I wondered if this new doctor recognized the psychological value of moral support by the owner for a sick cat. I asked if he allowed visiting privileges. "Oh, yes," said Dr. Perper, "It's better for a cat if he can see his owner every day." I felt reassured. "Maybe," I thought, "I've found a vet." It only remained to test him out if, heaven forbid, a real sickness should occur.

You will notice I was very careful not to tip my hand and let him know how important these questions were to me. I wanted to find out what his general attitude and policy was, not what he was going to do to get himself a client. I even went so far as to use my old stage name from my Broadway days in case he had heard of Anitra the cat groomer.

The Second Opinion

One thing you will have to test out later is the veterinarian's attitude about getting a second opinion. Whenever there is a question of a disease or any malfunction in the cat's body not responding to treatment, do not accept a verdict of "chronic" or "incurable" without seeking a second opinion from someone outside your own vet's office. This could be applied also to any case where surgery is suggested as long as the delay would not be considered dangerous to the cat.

I have several times over the years confronted Dr. Perper with my intention of taking a cat of mine or one of my clients' for a second opinion. Dr. Perper's response is always the same. He digs out the records of medications given, treatments tried, pulls out any X-rays, slips it all into a big envelope, and, as he hands it to me, he usually says, "Let me know what he says, I'd be interested." Here's a doctor who's always ready to learn something new. I've also often heard Dr. Perper conferring with other veterinarians by phone.

I can't work with a doctor who harbors a sense of competition or defensiveness over my desire to see if two heads might be better than one. More than once I've brought back to Dr. Perper a general confirmation of everything he said but with some little helpful suggestion about possible dietary treatment or physical therapy to try. Once you have the second opinion, be sure to give your doctor the information so your cat can benefit from the combined knowledge.

A last word about treatment: If the medicine your veterinarian prescribes doesn't seem to be doing any good, don't hesitate to call him or her at once and say so. Every living creature is different. There may be allergies and sensitivities to consider, or there may be a second disease lurking behind the primary one. Before you decide to change veterinarians, be sure you have given your present doctor every bit of information you have to help him or her diagnose accurately. Also, every medicine has some known side effects. If your cat has an adverse reaction such as diarrhea or excessive sleeping or panting, let the doctor know. The veterinarian is not a psychic; you have to call and tell him or her. He or she may just say that your cat's reaction is normal in the circumstances and thus put your mind to rest. The veterinarian is best equipped to judge whether or not to continue treatment or change to a different drug.

The Carrying Case

You should be able to weatherproof your cat's carrying case easily. This is difficult if you have the type with a lot of screen or grill-work suitable only for warm climates.

Let's assume for the sake of illustration, that (heaven forbid) your cat is taken ill in the middle of a snowstorm. Prepare the carrying case in the following way. First, fold two kitchen towels (or paper towels) to fit over the air holes in both ends of the case and tape them in place with masking tape. Also tape closed any additional holes in the case with masking tape. That way, air can filter in through the towel but the case will be breezeproof.

Now you need a plastic bottle. Empty your shampoo into a mixing bowl and fill your shampoo bottle with water as hot as you can handle. The hotter, the better. Screw on the lid and drop the bottle into a dirty sock. Thus you are providing both heat and the comfortable, familiar smell of your beloved foot. Fold a towel into the bottom of the case—

preferably a towel of a becoming color so it will subliminally affect the mind of the veterinarian and his or her assistant. (Some people prefer to use disposable diapers in the bottom of the case.) Drop the sock-covered bottle into the case.

Grab a large brown paper bag and a couple of cans of cat food in case the cat must stay overnight at the hospital. (Don't worry about the Vita-Mineral Mix now. This is an emergency, and you can always bring it along when you visit tomorrow if your cat does have to stay over at the veterinarian's.)

If you must transport your cat during a heat wave, use ice water in the shampoo bottle—or, better yet, a "dry ice pillow." Available in drugstores, this is a heavy plastic pillow filled with a liquid that freezes easily and is kept in the freezer for use on swellings or headaches—or to air condition pussycat carrying cases. Leave all the holes in the case open for more air circulation in summer, and be sure to wrap the ice bag in a towel so it doesn't come in direct contact with the cat.

Putting the Cat Into the Case

Before even looking at the cat, take three slow, deep breaths through your nose and remind yourself that your cat picks up your emotional vibrations. The three breaths will calm your mind. Just as your cat comforted you when your migraine lasted two days, you must now control your fears and nervousness sufficiently to provide truly honest reassurance. Let your mind dwell on the help and relief in store and how good it will be to find out just exactly what's wrong and be able to do something about it. Just before picking up the cat, put your hand into the box so that you feel how nice and warm (or cool) it is in there. As you pick your cat up and put him or her in, talk about that warmth. Say how you wish *you* were in a nice, warm box instead of having to walk out into that cold weather.

The proper way to put the cat in the carrying case is basically the same way you always put a cat down—front feet first. The second the cat's front feet touch the bottom of the box, slam the lid shut *on your own finger.* This accomplishes two things: speed and safety. You will be able to slam it shut rapidly and successfully because you will be secure in the knowledge that there is no possible chance of pinching the cat's tail. Gently extricate your finger as you tuck the tail, ear, or what-have-you inside. Grab the paper bag and cans of food, and off you go.

Hospitalization

If it turns out that the cat must be hospitalized, prepare the cage in the following manner: Take the brown paper bag, open it, and turn down a cuff all the way around the top. Do it slowly and carefully so that it never tears at all. The effect of this is to hold the bag open. Lay it inside the cage, thus providing a nice little cave of darkness and security the cat can crawl into to feel more secure. Hopefully this will prevent a frightened cat from cowering inside the litter box. Spread the towel on the bottom of the bag. Put fresh hot water in the hot water bottle, recover it with the sock, and slip it into the bag. Your object is to cushion a stressful situation in as many ways as possible. You've provided extra warmth with the hot water bottle, an illusion of security and an option of hiding with the paper bag, and your dear, familiar scent with your sock.

Take your leave casually. Here is an ideal time to use the ritual phrase that you always use when leaving your own home to signal a cat that this will be a short absence on your part. (See Chapter 1, the section called "Goodbye for Long or Short Periods.") For myself, when leaving in the morning for the day's work, my last words are always "See you later, Alligator" as opposed to, "OK, Purr, I'm leaving you in charge," which is what I say if I'm going to be away for the weekend or longer.

All that is left to do now is to extract an oath signed in blood by the vet that he or she will not provide hospital food—which is usually just as awful as the food we humans encounter in our own hospitals—but will use the food that you brought. Chances are either (1) the cat will not be hungry, or·(2) the cat will be required to fast preceding some hospital procedure. You may want to provide some special treats when you visit—such as chicken soup or steamed broccoli tops. You know what your cat loves. Discuss it with the vet. Just make sure that, at this time especially, it is top-quality nutrition. No Dorito Chips or rum raisin ice cream!

CHAPTER 9

The Cat and Its Human Family

Because my job entails going into people's homes to take care of their cats, I have a unique opportunity to observe at firsthand that delightful and complex interaction that takes place between the human family and its cats. I know so many of these families, and our relationship has extended now over so many years, that many common problems have been brought to my attention time and time again, which I will discuss in this chapter.

The New Baby

There are many old wives' tales about cats but the two concerning pregnancy and babies are the ones mentioned by newly pregnant women. Although they know these old wives' tales sound silly, a little reassurance is welcome to an expectant mother.

Several people have asked me if it's true that cleaning the litter box can cause a miscarriage. It sounds ridiculous, doesn't it? But, oddly enough, there *can* be a connection. Toxoplasmosis, the disease to which these people are referring, is a disease of rats, mice, and other rodents. For cats to carry the germs they must first have killed and eaten a rat, mouse, or forest rodent who had the disease. Then, if the cats do indeed contract the disease from this live prey there will be microscopic eggs in the stool. In order to pass it on to a human, the human must in turn ingest these eggs. That is to say—they must be eaten. Because they are in the stool, you might think that is impossible. But wait—what if, while cleaning the

175

litter box, some stool on the side of the box is touched by the owner's hand? If that person does not wash the hand carefully before picking up and eating a piece of food, that food could be contaminated inadvertently. Contamination could also occur after grooming cats or stroking the anal area. Unlikely as it sounds, pregnant women have been known to contract toxoplasmosis, and this disease *can* cause congenital defects or miscarriage. My advice has always been, "Why worry about it?—if the possibility is preying on your mind, simply drop a fresh stool sample off at your veterinarian and he or she will test it for you. And in the meantime, remember to wash your hands after cleaning the litter box."

The second old wives' tale has two variations, the most primitive being that cats like to suck the breath out of babies. The second variation is that the cat will smother the baby. Every time I hear of this slander, I think of little Matthew who was born into a household that already had four large cats. The cats ranged in temperament from lethargic to skittish, from friendly to withdrawn, and from playful to solitary. Both males and females were represented in this group.

From the time Matthew came home from the hospital, the cats loved to sleep with him in the crib. At first, three of the four cats were larger than Matthew. Just imagine what it must feel like to be small enough to snuggle your whole body against a cat's chest and be completely enveloped in that warm, soft, silkiness. Imagine being surrounded by the sound of a cat's purr. I don't know if the cats had anything to do with it, but Matthew was a very mellow and sunny baby. He was always grinning and gurgling.

When Matthew started to crawl, he would sometimes reach for the cats and try to grab hold of them. It was a simple matter for them to slip away from his grasp if they had had enough. They still continued to sleep with him.

During the crawling stage, Matthew and the cats really had a great time because at this point Matthew was almost as smart as the cats. The cats could understand him and play with him safely because Matthew had not yet reached the stage where he posed any sort of threat to the cats. He couldn't yet prevent the cats from leaving when they wanted to.

Matthew's mother knew that the toddler stage begins a time of transition, and the cats had to be protected. The time was approaching when Matthew would be strong enough to inadvertently harm a cat. A toddler may pick up a heavy toy and swing it about and accidentally hit the loving animal sitting close by. Toddlers are not yet capable of understanding that they now have superior strength and intelligence. More adult supervision was needed now until Matthew learned the rules involved in dealing with a pet.

Teach children the very first rule that will keep them safe for the rest of their lives: Never try to hold a cat if the cat wants to go. If you always let cats go, they will always come back to you. When dealing with strange cats (or dogs), never touch them with more than one hand at a time. That way it's clear to the animals that they are free to leave if they want to, and they won't feel threatened. As long as cats can leave if they want to, they will never have reason to scratch. Cats scratch only as a last resort if they are extremely upset and frightened.

Young Children

As children grow up, they will probably find the feeding and litter cleaning fascinating. Many children like to help with these activities, and I know several bright young people who have taken them over completely and have included even grooming in their list of accomplishments. This is one of the lovely contributions that your pets make to your children's welfare and personal growth. Just by their mere presence in the family, cats introduce the youngsters to a sense of responsibility.

However, the wise parent and loving owner never actually uses a helpless animal as a tool to teach children responsibility. Children may help with pet care—with the adult still in charge and overseeing. But even if the children are given full responsibility and think they are totally in charge, the aware adult will keep a constant, if surreptitious, check to see that each mealtime, each cleanup, each grooming session, and the condition of the litter box continue on the same high standards that prevailed before the younger family members took over. In other words— innocent pets must not be made to pay for children's forgetfulness or oversight. You, the parent, must maintain an ever-watchful eye.

A word to the wise—little children frequently hurt animals simply because they do not realize what constitutes pain or distress to an animal. Many children love cymbals and drums and cap pistols—however, such things could give a pussycat a heart attack. Cats are different from people, and it takes quite a while before children are old enough to understand that. (I might add—I've met many adults who still haven't reached that stage.)

Children raised in a loving household with pets will usually grow up to be loving owners. When remembering their own childhoods, what a pity it is if they have painful memories of their own cruelty to animals through ignorance or parental indulgence. The memories children will have when they grow up are being made now. Protect your children from painful memories by protecting the cat until the children are old enough to really understand.

Visitors in the Home

Not everyone owns or understands cats. Many a tragedy has struck because well-meaning friends or relatives or occasional workers come into a home and innocently open a window. If you expect workers to arrive while you are away, lock the cat in one room with litter and water and put a sign on the door that clearly states not to open the door or let the cat out. Most cats are afraid of workers, and a surprisingly large number of workers are afraid of or do not like cats. When friends and relatives come to visit, you can make sure that they know that care must be taken when opening or closing doors or drawers. You can also explain the danger of windows and make sure they know they should not play roughly with the cat with their hands.

Allergic to Cats?

I have frequently had the experience of people coming to visit who didn't know I had cats. Several times those people have told me that they were always allergic to cats and cannot understand why they were not having a reaction to mine. It's nice to be able to help such people understand the reasons by explaining how diet and feeding patterns cut down dander, which is the substance they are allergic to. (See Chapter 2, on "Diet.")

I remember Marcie and Lou Gustavson, a nice young couple who moved in down the hall. Lou was highly allergic to cats, as well as to a number of other things. Marcie had always lived with cats and missed them terribly, so one evening they came over to visit me and my cats. I had eleven cats in residence at the time: my own three, a couple of convalescents boarding for nursing care, and six adoptables. Both Marcie and Lou had a great time petting and hugging and playing with all the cats.

Lou reasoned that he could always leave if his eyes started to itch or if he had trouble breathing. When Lou had no allergic response, Marcie immediately began to wonder if perhaps all was not lost as far as Lou and cats being able to live together. She asked hopefully if I thought they could try adopting a couple of cats if she kept the cats strictly to the diet I suggested and removed the food between meals. I felt a bit hesitant about committing myself. I'd never tried to solve this particular problem before, and I certainly didn't want to disappoint Marcie. But, because I had so many cats up for adoption, I decided that we should give it the old college try.

I told them that we'd have a much better chance of success if we not only controlled the amount of dander on the cat but also tried to lessen Lou's allergic reaction. They were all for that, of course. Because allergies are evidence of a faulty immunological response, I have found that housecleaning a clogged intestinal tract goes a long way toward alleviating the condition, at least partially. I wanted to give us a wider margin within which to work.

After explaining this, I asked Lou if he would make some changes in his own diet. Drawing from my experience with yoga and macrobiotics, I told him to eliminate eggs, pork, and white sugar from his diet. I also asked him to eat fish instead of red meats, and cut down on butter and other dairy products. I asked him to add one-fourth cup of bran and a tablespoonful of lecithin granules to his diet each day and to eat as many raw vegetables as possible.

He was game to try. When I asked them if they had any special cats in mind, they just looked at each other and smiled. Lou said, "I think we'd like to take 'the married couple.'" I couldn't believe my luck. "The married couple"—Sally and Victor—were two short-haired black cats who had been waiting for adoption for several months.

When I got her, Sally was the smallest cat I ever saw in my life. She was nine years old, and she did not even tip the scale at four pounds. She had arrived when her owner left her, supposedly for boarding, and was never heard from again. I soon found out why. Sally immediately began defecating all over the apartment. She was in sad shape. She had been declawed and was a veritable walking snowdrift of dandruff. She crouched morosely inside an empty cat food carton, hurling threats at any cat who came too close. None of the other cats liked her. So she just sat there frowning, all hunched up in a ball. I wondered how in the world I was ever going to get rid of this one. Who in their right mind would want to adopt an angry pile of dandruff who defecated all over the place?

Dr. Perper diagnosed her as having colitis and I started adjusting and experimenting with her diet until I found that the basic super finicky owner's "I'll-Do-Anything-for-My-Cat" Diet plus one-half teaspoon bran conditioned her stool so she didn't have to either strain or suddenly let go wherever she was. Of course, this high-quality diet, which was specifically adjusted for her particular intestinal needs, immediately had its effect on the dandruff. Teeny tiny little Sally developed a plushy coat in two months flat. But she still huddled morosely in her box most of the time.

Four-year-old Victor came strolling onto the scene in the company of two other cats, all of whom had been left ownerless when an elderly client had been taken to the hospital with a heart attack and never returned. Victor was as big as Sally was tiny. He was the very picture of shiny black health and vigor. His owner had had the cats on a high-quality diet for over two years. Victor spotted Sally from the doorway when he entered. He just strolled over, jaunty and jolly. "Hi, good looking," he seemed to be saying as he stretched himself out next to Sally's carton. Sally cowered back, muttering swear noises but I noticed she didn't show her fangs and I saw her blink a couple of times, a sure sign that her heart was not entirely made of ice. I think Victor was a gift from the compassionate cat goddess to Sally. He was so mellow and sweet that nobody could resist him—human or animal.

By the second day, Sally and Victor were an item. Victor moved into Sally's carton, and there was a great deal of mutual licking and close cuddling. After Victor's arrival, Sally was seen more and more at large in the room. Victor was the leader, but Sally did follow and leave her cloistered bower. As I watched the romance unfolding, the question was never far from my mind as to how in the world I would ever get them adopted together. It's hard enough to find a home for one cat—opportunities for placing two together are almost nonexistent. I had been steeling myself for the day when I would have to break up Sally and Victor. It was not a happy prospect.

Then into my life walked this nice young couple who announced they'd like to take the two of them. On top of that, from the looks on their faces, I could see that they were already falling in love with my Sally and Victor. Obviously the Gustavsons were a second gift from the cat goddess.

At the end of the month, Marcie called to report that Lou had found his tendency to allergic reactions in general to have lessened. They were anxious to come over and pick up the cats, both of them feeling very positive that all would go well. Lou had lost five pounds during that first month on the new diet and, incidentally, a year later he still declares that he feels better than he has for a long time. His allergy to cats seems to be completely controlled. And Apartment 5J now boasts not one but two married couples.

Taking the Cat Along: Vacations, Visits, and Moving

Because cats are such territorial animals, loving sameness the way they do, uprooting them and moving them around can be a traumatic event. However, if uprooting them means that they can then be with you, their beloved owner, that is better than leaving them behind. The thing to do is try it a few times and find out how well it works for you and your cats. For the best chance of success and a smooth transition, start preparing in advance. Leave the carrying case out for at least a few hours a day so they can sniff it and get used to it. Many cats will nap in the carrier. It is a nice size and shape for napping. Throw the weekly catnip party inside the carrier. If your cat has a favorite treat such as olives, cantaloupe, sweet corn, or so on, feed him that particular tidbit inside the carrier once or twice. This way you're creating all sorts of happy associations connected with the carrier.

The case should not be too large. The perfect size is just large enough so your cat can stand on all fours and turn around. If the case is too large, the cat tends to slide around. I like the ones that have clear plastic domes, so the cat can see out. You can always drape a towel over the dome if your cat wants privacy.

Review how to place the cat in the carrier by reading through the pertinent section in Chapter 8, "Going to the Vet."

When the day of the journey arrives, withhold all food and water after midnight of the night before. Skipping breakfast is not one-quarter as traumatic as it would be if the cat dirtied inside the carrier. Whatever your mode or modes of transportation, your safest bet is to leave the carrier closed the whole time, although if traveling by plane they'll probably ask you to open it at the inspection point before you get on the plane. Ask the inspector to allow you to open it in a room where you can shut or lock the door.

Once comfortably seated in your conveyance, you may consider opening the case so that your furry friend can stretch a little, look around, and get a little more reassurance from you. This sometimes works very well. Again, the only way to find out is to try it. The thing to keep in mind is not to open the case all the way until you have a firm grip on the cat. Make sure you keep your hold on the cat in such a way that at any moment you can easily close the case again. In other words, do not allow the cat to put paws up on the edge of the case. Let the cat sit on your lap inside the open case, and you can put your arms into the case and wrap them around him or her.

As always, when introducing any new activity to the cat, your attitude and mental vibrations are all important. If you are nervous about putting the cat into the case, your cat will be nervous about getting into the case. If you are nervous about flying, your cat will feel apprehensive about flying. Keep your mind centered on the comforts of your cat's situation—how secure the case is and how pleasant it is to be in a case and be carried. Put a nice soft towel in the bottom of the case plus a small piece of your clothing such as a sock or glove to provide additional comfort. Don't allow anyone to rap on the case or call to your cat. When cats are confined in a case and cannot run away, it is definitely not the time to confront them with strangers.

I think the watchword is casualness. Try to keep your feelings casual about everything. If you get all upset because the ticket was made out wrong, cats will pick up your emotions, and, because they don't know about tickets, they will assume that some danger threatens.

A word about shipping your cat in the baggage compartment. I understand it's the only way they'll take an animal on the train. Insist on inspecting the baggage car to find out about the temperature factor, making suitable arrangements if need be—hot water bottle in the case if it's winter; cold water bottle if it's summer—and try to secure visiting privileges if the trip lasts more than a couple of hours.

As for sending your pet in the luggage compartment on the airplane, I have never done it because, frankly, I am afraid. I know people who have done it with no ill effects to their pets. On the other hand, I have also heard of pets arriving dead or near death. They were frozen to death from the high altitudes or brain damaged from a lack of oxygen. More than once, heavy baggage has crashed against the carrier, springing it open and releasing hysterical animals to run loose among the baggage until the owner could be summoned to help capture them.

If you know you're going to travel by plane, the easiest way that several of my clients have found is to buy a seat for your pet. Granted, this is quite expensive. So, if you want to avoid this expense, make your reservations very early and secure "pet permission" when you do. Insist that you will only accept a booking that includes pet permission and that you want it *in writing* because you refuse to allow your pet to travel with the baggage.

Pet permission on the airlines is available for one pet per compartment per flight. Once you get pet permission, the airline may then insist that you buy a special carrier that fits underneath the seat. I cannot caution you strongly enough—get that carrier in advance.

My friend and co-author Norma had to fly with her cat Clarence when she was returning to New York after a season of winter stock at a theater in Florida. She tried gently putting Clarence into the case just to see if he would fit because it looked so small. She admits that she was having serious doubts and that her mind was not tranquil about it. Clarence became totally hysterical, yowling and ripping at the case, so she let him out at once. Norma then considered sending him in the plane's luggage compartment, but Clarence had been ailing and just the thought of his riding there upset her. Various friends gave conflicting advice, and because Norma had had no direct experience before, she resolved in desperation to ask Clarence one more time. She sat down with him and opened the case on the bed. Very slowly, very clearly, and in great detail, she explained to Clarence the pros and cons of the two alternatives. Then she told him how she felt and how much nicer it would be for her to have him close to her on the trip.

Then she looked into Clarence's eyes and told him very clearly that she wanted to try it just one more time. She picked him up, laid him on his side inside the carrier, and firmly closed the lid. This time Clarence didn't say a word but just lay there waiting for Norma to make the next move, whatever that might be. She opened the case, and Clarence sat up, stretched, and stepped out in a dignified manner. He succeeded in reassuring Norma that the carrying case would be OK.

Before the day of the flight friends who saw the case, squat and tiny as it was, and saw Clarence, large and sprawling as he was, gave the opinion that shutting a monster like Clarence in "that little thing" was tantamount to cruelty. Norma had fresh misgivings, vacillating in her mind between the tiny airline carrying case and the great unknown luggage compartment. But in the end she stuck by Clarence's decision, as she had promised him she would.

When travel day arrived, sure enough—Clarence kept his side of the bargain. As Norma chatted about the positive aspects of the trip, Clarence curled himself down in that cheap little plastic monstrosity and said not a word when the lid was closed. Norma continued to talk about how nice it would be to be home, mentioning Clarence's favorite sunny windowsill where he has his own special view of New York's pigeons. On the way to the airport, Norma was sharing a cab with her friend Jennie, and guilt feelings kept creeping into her mind about Clarence's cramped accommodations. Jennie, a cat owner herself, said she thought Clarence looked quite smug and content. "You know how cats like to crawl into tight little places," she said. "It makes them feel safe." Of course, Jennie was perfectly right, and a great load of guilt and apprehension lifted from Norma's mind. Norma and Clarence were free to enjoy the fun parts of the trip. About 98 percent of the time, with about 98 percent of the cats, if you feel happy and secure and satisfied about the way your pets are traveling, they will too.

Try traveling without giving your cat tranquilizers before you resort to them. Tranquilizers are debilitating to the cat's system—they are just not very good for cats. They lower resistance to disease. If you decide you must use one, get them from a veterinarian who knows your cats and allow enough time to try out the dosage at least three separate times before the actual travel day arrives. Every cat is different, and if the dosage is not just right a cat may have a hyperreaction: The tranquilizer, instead of calming, can render the cat quite hysterical. So you must work out the dose in advance. Remember, feeding or not feeding before the journey also changes the amount of tranquilizer needed. So take that into consideration while you are trying to work out the proper dose for your animal.

Visiting a New Place

When you arrive, remember how territorially conscious cats are and how uneasy they are with new people and places. You can cushion an otherwise stressful situation by limiting the number of new things they must deal with. First of all, confine the cats in a small space such as the bedroom and bathroom. Even if you're visiting your great grandmother in her three-story farmhouse, don't let them explore until they have spent at least one night in the restricted territory and become familiar with it. Before you open their cases, set up the old, familiar litter box and their own food and water dish so they will see that their personal necessities are there for them. Try to spend at least a half hour in that territory with them, and leave some of your personal belongings with your smell on them lying about before you leave them. In this way, you reassure them that you're coming back. Hopefully you will have brought their favorite toys, and before you leave you can reassure them even further if you run through their favorite games a couple of times, just as you always do at home.

So, after you have given them their own familiar things and strewn a few of your own familiar possessions about the room, and played their old, familiar games, you can leave with a light heart, knowing that they will probably spend a fascinating hour exploring new territory and then fall asleep.

The next day, if you decide to let them increase their territory, make sure that you explore it first for dangers such as unscreened windows and poisonous plants or chemicals. Then you may wish to increase the territory gradually, a few rooms at a time. Be sure that everyone who enters and leaves the house knows that your cats are running around loose and that people must be careful about closet doors, drawers, and certainly the door to the outside. You and your host may well decide on certain areas to which they will not be admitted, such as a damp cellar, a dusty attic, or certainly an unscreened balcony.

If you stay in a hotel, you must put a sign on the door cautioning all who enter not to let the cats out. It's always good to speak to your maid personally, making sure that she understands the situation clearly and that she's not afraid of cats. In some instances, it's wiser to arrange to pick up your own clean linens at the desk rather than chance a maid or bell-man unthinkingly opening a window or door.

If you're moving into a new home, the thing to do to keep stress to a minimum is to surround the cats with familiarity and keep them away from the area of upheaval as much as possible. In other words, on the last couple of days before the move, when packing and bustle reaches its height and when you are the busiest, confine them to your bedroom and have the packing boxes in the living room and the kitchen. Leave a few pieces of clothing that you have worn lying around in there so that they have the comfort of your scent even while you're busy elsewhere. If the premoving bustle outside the bedroom becomes noisy, turn on the radio or television in the bedroom and let is play softly. Put in a short appearance every hour or so, letting them feel that you are calm and satisfied and pleased that they are there in the bedroom.

On the actual moving day, the best plan is to confine the cats to some room that the movers will not enter. This may be a bathroom. Give them their litter and water, their favorite toys, a piece of your clothing, and perhaps a cardboard box or brown paper bag to hide in or play in as a special treat. Put a sign on the bathroom door, and have it locked, if possible. Here again, keep your attitude casual. Emphasize to them the fun they'll have playing in the paper bag. Don't think about the fact that they're closed off in the bathroom. Tell them how lucky they are to be able to rest quietly here while you deal with those noisy movers.

The cats should arrive at the new home only after you have at least one room pretty well settled where you can confine them. They'll see the old, familiar furniture and feel reassured. Just as when you are visiting someone else's house, let them get used to one or two rooms first and then add to their territory a couple of rooms each day. Don't forget to check your new home carefully before you let the cats explore it. Be sure that it is just as safe and cat-proof as their old home was.

While You're Away

Sara and Dan were going to be away for two weeks. They were worried about what to do with their beloved Midnight while they were gone— hire a daily sitter; take him to stay with Norma, who already had a cat; ask Aunt Dot, who doesn't have a cat, to keep him; or board him with a veterinarian? I heard nothing about it until two days before they were scheduled to leave.

I said, right off, that boarding with a veterinarian was not a good idea. Even if they board Midnight with one who lets the cats out for a walk twice a day up and down the halls, it's still a small cage. And veterinarian's offices are, of course, full of sick cats breathing germs into the air. Cats who come there are in trouble, in pain, and frightened. The vibes are stressful.

Aunt Dot might be OK because she has no other animals, especially if she already knows and loves Midnight. You'd have to be certain, though, that her windows were screened and she wouldn't let him out. And you'd have to be sure to supply her with the correct food and the Vita-Mineral Mix. Then you wouldn't have to give a lecture on feline nutrition but only a five-minute talk on the evils of leaving food available between meals.

The absence of the two owners is the first stress factor. And being placed in a new environment is Stress Number Two. Therefore, Sara and Dan should give Midnight additional vitamins—double the Vita-Mineral Mix and add 500 units of vitamin C daily for two days before leaving. If Aunt Dot is amenable to pilling Midnight, it would be valuable for him to have the vitamin C for the first five days of his stay. There are new germs at Aunt Dot's that he didn't have in his own environment—a different ratio of germs and viruses for him to deal with. And the stresses will lower his resistance; the Vita-Mineral Mix and vitamin C will help bolster it a little.

Norma's cat, Clarence, is an old sweetie pie. I personally would love to spend two weeks with Clarence. But Midnight will not be aware that Clarence is an old sweetie pie. To him, Clarence will simply constitute a great big Stress Number Three—a strange cat. Midnight will feel he is invading "strange cat's" territory. Moreover, instead of the strange new germs he would encounter in a no-cat household, he will encounter a different balance of cat germs at Clarence's house.

Of course, if Midnight is a physically strong robust cat, the pros could outweigh the cons as far as leaving him with Norma and Clarence. Norma is a cat care expert, and Midnight would have the comfort of her companionship as opposed to being left alone. Then, too, Midnight and Clarence might just form such a warm and wonderful friendship that his stay might very well be like sending a child to summer camp. There are always a lot of unknown variables to deal with when working with living creatures.

The safest and most usual way to deal with the situation is hiring a sitter. The only sitters I trust are my own, but we cost $7 a visit, and that's a lot of money for two weeks. By hiring a sitter, Stress Number Three is not encountered, but Stress Number Four is—and that's the growing loneliness. I feel very sorry for single cats. Every time a cat is left alone, after a certain amount of time, he or she begins to expect you. If you usually come home at 5 P.M., then at 5:30 your cat begins to worry. By 6, your cat will assume that you have been killed by predators and will begin to mourn. It is quite a strain for a pussycat to be left alone for two weeks with a sitter appearing only one hour a day.

If only Midnight had a friend, he would never again have to face the horror of being alone. Cats are group animals. They live in prides. When they are together, the worst of terrors are lessened. "Our humans may have met with an accident but together we'll work it out—we'll muddle through somehow, together"; "At least we'll be warm, together"; "Together we can play." Hopefully, by the second day they will begin to expect the sitter, who cleans the litter, supplies the food, and spends the remainder of the hour cuddling, grooming, and/or playing.

So if Midnight is to be left alone in the apartment, extra care must be taken to give him reassurance and to distract and entertain him. The first two days, the sitter should come twice a day instead of once. This will hasten Midnight's acceptance of the sitter and quickly build the new pattern of sitter, food, and fun. Dan and Sara should arrange for the sitter to come twice on two or three other days if he or she deems it advisable. They should be sure to leave the carry case out, leave the food and can opener in plain sight, and leave a note listing:

- Your telephone number
- The telephone number of a close friend or relative in the immediate neighborhood who also has a key
- The veterinarian's phone number
- Instructions for feeding
- Any instructions for medication
- Where to find toys, grooming tools, and catnip

Midnight must be distracted from his loneliness. A toy left lying around all the time is no longer exciting. Catnip, if given every day, becomes a bore. So Sara and Dan should not give catnip for two weeks before they leave. And they should gather up all his toys the day before they go, leaving only one toy on the floor.

Dan and Sara should instruct the sitter to rotate the toys, giving Midnight a different one each day so that each toy is taken away from him before it becomes stale. They should leave one large brown paper bag for each week they will be gone. Then one day a week, instead of the toy, the brown paper bag can be opened and thrown on the floor for him to play with. The next day can be catnip day, putting the catnip inside of or on top of the brown paper bag—excitement on excitement. The following day the sitter can take it away and rotate a different toy.

To give Midnight the feeling that the apartment is not deserted, the sitter should leave a different light on each night and alternate days with the radio on and the radio off (this also discourages burglars). A small pile of dirty laundry can be left in the corner of the bedroom, and Midnight should be able to get into the bedroom closet and sit on the shoes.

I have several thoughtful clients who leave special food treats for their cats, to assuage their own guilt about leaving for vacation or business trips. Constance leaves barbecued chicken. Caroline leaves sliced turkey; Mrs. Aparicio, miniature shrimp. If I were leaving any of my cats all alone, I'd leave a couple of broiled chicken thighs and, for Priscilla, some baby food oatmeal and half-and-half.

All these things can be fed along with the other food, not exclusively. You don't want to throw the nutrition out of balance along with all the other stress factors.

I have several clients who like to call once a week to assure themselves that all is going well. Usually there is some little thing you want to check on. Is he having a stool every day? If not, the Metamucil is in the bathroom cabinet. Is he eating? If not, there's baby food in the small cabinet over the refrigerator.

Remember, there are much worse things that can happen to a cat than your going away for two weeks. Granted, it's hard, but at least he or she has shelter and food.

But what if you could cut the stress factor by 50 percent? What if you could really relax, secure in the knowledge that your Midnight is having a ball? It's easy. Get him a friend. Someone to train in his own pawprints. Someone to get into trouble with when your back is turned. Even if you work at home and you're home twenty-four hours a day, and you adore your cat, and your cat adores you, think of it this way: What if you were owned by two of the most wonderful elephants in the world? You love them dearly, and they dote on your every move. They give you the very best food, they give you everything that you want plus a few extra things you never thought of to surprise and delight you. In short, they give you everything your heart could possibly desire except . . . another human. Need I say more?

Bibliography

Davis, Adelle. *Let's Get Well*. New York: Harcourt Brace Jovanovich, 1965.

Davis, Adelle. *Let's Eat Right to Keep Fit*. New York: Harcourt Brace Jovanovich, 1970.

Gallico, Paul. *The Abandoned*. New York: Knopf, 1950.

Lappé, Frances Moore. *Diet for a Small Planet*. New York: Ballantine, 1971.

Lorenz, Konrad. *King Solomon's Ring*. New York: Crowell, 1952.

Lorenz, Konrad. *On Aggression*. New York: Harcourt Brace Jovanovich, 1974.

Maltz, Maxwell. *Psycho-Cybernetics*. Englewood Cliffs, N.J.: Prentice-Hall, 1960.

Muramoto, Naboru. *Healing Ourselves*. St. Louis: Formur International, 1973.

Ohsawa, George. *Macrobiotics: An Invitation to Health and Happiness*. Ohsawa Foundation, 1434 Corson, Los Angeles, 1971.

Sivananda, Swami Paramahansa. *Yoga, Health and Diet*. Rishikesh, India: Yoga-Vedanta, Forest Academy, 1958.

Prevention Magazine. 33 East Minor Street, Emmaus, PA 18049.

Wilbourn, Carole C. *Cat Talk*. New York: Macmillan, 1979.

Wilbourn, Carole C. *The Inner Cat*. Briarcliff Manor, N.Y.: Stein and Day, 1978.

Index